YEARBOOK

2006

THE BEST & WORST OF THE YEAR

TABLE OF CONTENTS 2005

EDITOR Cutler Durkee **CREATIVE DIRECTOR** Rina Migliaccio **ART DIRECTOR** Dwayne Shaw **PHOTO DIRECTOR** Donna Cohen **WRITERS** Steve Dougherty, Jamie Bufalino, Michelle Tan, Erica Sóuter, Jill Smolowe, Michelle Tauber, Michael Lipton, Eleni Gage, Marisa Wong **DESIGNERS** David Schlow, David Jaenisch, William McDermott **REPORTERS** Lisa Kay Greissinger (Chief), Hugh McCarten, Beth Perry, Olivia Abel, Jennifer Wren, Paula Kashtan, Daniel Levy, Lisa Helem, Melody Wells, Ashley Williams, Jane Sugden, Samantha McIntyre **PHOTO ASSISTANT** Donna Tsufura **COPY EDITORS** Alan Levine, Lance Kaplan **SPECIAL THANKS TO** Elaine Francisco, Robert Britton, Céline Wojtala, Sal Covarrúbias, Margery Frohlinger, Charles Nelson, Susan Radlauer, Annette Rusin, Ean Sheehy, Jack Styczynski, Patrick Yang

Time Inc. Home Entertainment **PUBLISHER** Richard Fraiman **EXECUTIVE DIRECTOR, MARKETING SERVICES** Carol Pittard **DIRECTOR, RETAIL & SPECIAL SALES** Tom Mifsud **MARKETING DIRECTOR, BRANDED BUSINESSES** Swati Rao **DIRECTOR, NEW PRODUCT DEVELOPMENT** Peter Harper **FINANCIAL DIRECTOR** Steven Sandonato **PREPRESS MANAGER** Emily Rabin **MARKETING MANAGER** Laura Adam **BOOK PRODUCTION MANAGER** Suzanne Janso **ASSOCIATE PREPRESS MANAGER** Anne-Michelle Gallero **ASSOCIATE MARKETING MANAGER** Danielle Radano **SPECIAL THANKS TO** Bozena Bannett, Alexandra Bliss, Glenn Buonocore, Robert Marasco, Brooke McGuire, Jonathan Polsky, Chavaughn Raines, Ilene Schreider, Adriana Tierno, Britney Williams

HELL &HIGH WATER

Slammed and swamped by the mother
of all hurricanes, the shattered Gulf
Coast struggles to recover

Volunteer Paul Mire of Destrehan, La., helped rescue stranded New Orleans residents on Sept. 1.

In what may be the worst natural disaster in American history, Hurricane Katrina exploded onto the Gulf Coast before dawn on Aug. 29, unleashing tornado-force winds, devastating storm surges, torrential rains and deadly floods. The unprecedented storm wiped out entire towns, made temporarily uninhabitable one of the nation's most storied cities, New Orleans, and cut an apocalyptic swath through Louisiana, Mississippi, Alabama and Florida. Katrina left more than a thousand dead, more than a million homeless and at least $70 billion in damage. "This," said A.J. Holloway, mayor of hard-hit Biloxi, Miss., "is our tsunami."

As survivors struggled to cope, and countless Gulf Coast residents were relocated hundreds and even thousands of miles from home, the collateral damage included faith in the power of government and the abilities of the nation's leaders—most famously the President, whose initial apparent lack of engagement shocked many— to come to the aid of its people in a time of great need. And yet, while Katrina's devastating impact and horrific aftermath forced Americans to confront uncomfortable truths about the country's economic and racial divides, the grit of many victims survived the test. "We lost everything," said Penny Dean, 50, of Pearlington, Miss. "But I'm determined to get my life back. I want to look back on Katrina with a feeling of triumph—to say she tried to beat us down, but we wouldn't let her."

Katrina's toll: After the floods came fires, difficult to fight with the water system shut down.

Survivors clung to lifelines of every sort in the storm's wake.

'I STILL HEAR VOICES SCREAMING AT ME, SAYING, "HELP ME, HELP ME." I KNOW WE COULDN'T SAVE EVERYONE, BUT I WON'T EVER FORGET THE SCREAMING'
—NEW ORLEANS RESCUE VOLUNTEER BILLY RHODES, 18

TSUNAMI

Despite massive relief efforts, the tidal wave's survivors struggle to cope

"A big wave came," reads the poem written by a 10-year-old girl named Sufrisah, who was orphaned and left homeless in the aftermath of the Indian Ocean tsunami that killed her parents and wiped out her fishing village in the Indonesian province of Aceh. "It came with anger."

And left almost unimaginable destruction in its wake. Triggered by an earthquake that erupted on the ocean's floor on the day after Christmas, 2004—one so immense that it altered the Earth's rotation—deadly tsunami waves engulfed the coastlines of 12 countries, killing more than 240,000 people. Victims of the brutally egalitarian waves included wealthy tourists at pricey seaside resorts as well as the poorest villagers. "Suddenly a huge wave smashed into our backs," recalled an Indian fisherman's wife who later found the body of her 9-year-old son on the beach. "His head was buried in the sand. I knew it was him because of his striped blue-and-white T-shirt and his gray trousers. I crouched by his side and wept." With more than $1 billion raised in the U.S. alone for disaster relief, the world's response was heartening.

Yet months after the disaster, Sufrisah, like thousands of other orphaned children, faced an uncertain future. Living in one of 21 UNICEF child centers in Aceh where 3,000 other young victims are cared for, Sufrisah goes nowhere without the two backpacks that contain all her worldly possessions. She keeps them close, she said, "so nothing can wash them away."

Scenes of sorrow: a child's body, uncovered in a makeshift morgue in Banda Aceh, Indonesia, and (above) the remains of a Phi Phi Island hotel in Thailand.

A difficult year started smoothly for the President and First Lady (dancing at the Inaugural Commander-in-Chief Ball on Jan. 20).

SECOND TERM, FIRST STEPS

For a few brief moments, as the year began, the President and First Lady made it all look easy

I intend to bring people together to do big things for the country," President Bush said before his Jan. 20 inauguration. Top on his list of goals were "Social Security reform, legal reform and [to] continue to work on education reforms." Even presidents, of course, don't always get what they want: By year's end Social Security reform was floundering, and the White House was coping with a messier Iraq war, the political aftershocks of Hurricane Katrina and the indictment of vice presidential aide Lewis Libby. One inaugural unveiling that *did* stand the test of time: First Lady Laura Bush's slimmer self (she had dropped 20 lbs., to a size 8) and looser, more casual hairstyle—a switch from what her own daughters had once compared to a helmet.

"We exited this relationship as beautifully as we entered it," Aniston (with Pitt in 2004) initially said of their separation.

THE SPLIT HEARD ROUND THE WORLD

When Hollywood golden couple Jennifer Aniston and Brad Pitt announced that they were going their separate ways after seven years together, it marked the not-so-happy ending of a beloved storybook romance

Once the initial shock wore off—the bombshell came Jan. 7 when Hollywood's golden couple, Brad Pitt and Jennifer Aniston, announced their separation in PEOPLE—it looked like they might pull off the improbable: a low-key high-profile Hollywood divorce. Maybe they weren't destined to be the Gen X Bogart and Bacall, but they seemed determined that the split would be choreographed with the same grace that made their 2000 nuptials a delight.

"We happily remain committed and caring friends with great love and affection for one another," they said in a joint statement. "For those who follow these sort of things," they added with knowing good humor, "we would like to explain that our separation is not the result of any of the speculation reported by the tabloid media."

That speculation, of course, had centered around Angelina Jolie, Pitt's costar in the soon-to-be-blockbuster *Mr. & Mrs.*

Smith. There was nothing to the rumors, the couple's friends insisted. "Brad is a very monogamous person," said a colleague. "He doesn't stray." And yet a friend of the couple's said, "Jennifer knew that Angelina got under his skin, and it bothered her."

That Pitt's infatuation with Jolie was more than tattoo-deep became resoundingly clear in April, when the two were photographed, along with her adopted son Maddox, on the beach at a romantic seaside resort in Africa, where Jolie was on a humanitarian mission for the U.N. Those, and subsequent public displays of non-platonic affection by the pair, prompted Aniston's surprisingly candid *Vanity Fair* comments in August. "The world was shocked and I was shocked," she said of evidence that seemed to undermine Pitt's assurance to a friend that "this is not about another woman."

Interspersed with Rachel-worthy one-liners ("Billy Idol called," she quipped about Pitt's then-blond locks. "He wants his look back"), Aniston said that her "sensitivity chip"-challenged ex caused her "moments of anger, of hurt, of embarrassment." Yet, she added, life without Brad wasn't all pity parties and lonely walks on the beach. "I'm excited about what the future holds," said Aniston, who was then commuting between her home in Malibu and Chicago, where she and Vince Vaughn were filming *The Break Up.* "Maybe it's a fairy tale," she said of true love, "but I believe in happily ever after."

'HE JUST WASN'T THERE FOR ME'
—JENNIFER ANISTON, ON PITT, WHO DIDN'T ATTEND HER EMOTIONAL FINAL *FRIENDS* TAPING (TO *VANITY FAIR*)

On Jan. 6 Pitt and Aniston strolled the beach on Anguilla, where they spent the New Year holiday with pals Courteney Cox and David Arquette. The next day they announced their split.

MOVING ON

For Brad, Angelina; for Jen—at least for now—her Vince valiant

The rumors began to fly almost as soon as the cameras started rolling on *Mr. & Mrs. Smith* in January, 2004. And while his attraction to his famously seductive costar was obvious even to his wife and her friends—"There was a connection, and he was honest about that with Jen," Courteney Cox told *Vanity Fair*—the pair adamantly denied that they became romantically involved at that time. "He didn't do anything while he was married," a source told PEOPLE. "He'll go to the grave saying that."

After the split was announced it was a different matter. First, Angelina and Brad posed in some campy, provocative photographs for lensman Steven Klein for a *W* feature titled "Domestic Bliss"; weeks later, in shots seen round the world, Brad and Angelina seemed to be living the dream on a Kenyan beach. Brad later accompanied her to Ethiopia when she adopted her daughter Zahara; since then the two have been photographed together often by paparazzi, although they have never made an official public appearance together or acknowledged they are a couple.

"I adore Vince Vaughn, but I'm not going out with Vince Vaughn. I barely know the guy." So Jennifer Aniston told *Vanity Fair*, truthfully no doubt, in the summer when she and Vaughn began shooting *The Break Up*, a film to which she was bringing immeasurable, if unwanted, expertise. But just a week after her divorce became final Oct. 2, Aniston and Vaughn (in Chicago, above) went public. Snuggling under a blanket on the terrace of Chicago's NoMI restaurant, the pair made no attempt to keep their romance under wraps. "She was all wrapped up with that guy she's supposedly not dating," an on-looker said dryly. Seen "kissing and making out" at other Windy City nightspots, the two spent a week together touring his hometown (he even took Jen to meet his mom) to almost universal applause. "She couldn't have picked a better person to spend a few months with while she's going through all this," pal Jason Bateman told *Elle*. "Vince brings out something in Jennifer that brightens her," said a source. "She's constantly belly-laughing when they're together. It's a joy to see."

KIRSTIE ALLEY

Shedding 55 lbs. and counting, she's a *Fat Actress* no more

A te massive quantities of Santa-head frosted sugar cookies, cheese fondue, steak tartare, key lime pie, home-made chicken and noodles, with Cinnabon chaser and 50 or 60 other mystery foods. Then went to dinner." A typical entry in Kirstie Alley's diary-like memoir *How to Lose Your Ass and Regain Your Life* chronicles a 2004 growth spurt that saw her weight balloon, she said, to 203 lbs. By March, when her book's release coincided with the premiere of her Showtime comedy series *Fat Actress*, she had shed more than 20. "We'll see if anyone hits on me," she said on her way into the launch party in late February. "If they do, I'm going to put out. It's going to be an exciting night."

Six months later she had lost another 30 lbs. But as much as she enjoyed her new svelte self, there was a downside to her disappearing act: She doesn't expect Showtime to renew her series. "I think [the network execs] have great concerns with me not being fat," she said.

JOHN ROBERTS

After a surprisingly quiet confirmation, a most exclusive club gets a new chief

Judge John Roberts

When President Bush announced 50-year-old John Roberts's nomination to replace retiring Supreme Court Justice Sandra Day O'Connor during a live broadcast from the White House, Roberts was upstaged by one of his two young children, who danced a jig in front of the gathered media. But even before Roberts got the chance to be confirmed as the latest addition to the Court, he nabbed a promotion: Following the Sept. 3 death of Chief Justice William Rehnquist, Bush tapped Roberts to replace him. Although many in Washington expected Roberts's nomination to set off a confrontation, in the end he was confirmed by the Senate with relative ease. "I come before this committee with no agenda, no platform," he said. "I will approach every case with an open mind." He gaveled the Court to order Oct. 3.

LOST AND FOUND

Quick thinking by a wily Denny's waitress helps rescue a missing child

Hope had dwindled that the children, missing since their mother and brother were murdered in a horrific May 16 massacre in Coeur d'Alene, Idaho, would be found alive. But in the wee hours of July 2, waitress Amber Deahn, 24, recognized Shasta Groene, 8, with a middle-aged man at a local Denny's. Thanks to Deahn, who dawdled filling their order to buy time while her supervisor called police, Shasta was rescued and her alleged captor, Joseph Duncan III, 42, was arrested and later charged with the May 16 murders. Sadly, no more miracles were in store. The remains of brother Dylan, 9, were discovered July 10. "She's worried about whether this guy could chase her again," Steven Groene, 48, said of his daughter. "We assure her he will not brutalize any more children."

THE DOVE GIRLS

A clever campaign made six average-size women the biggest thing in advertising

When these nonwaif women posed in their underwear for a ubiquitous Dove skin-cream ad last summer, not everyone joined in the chorus of praise. "If I want to see plump gals baring too much skin, I'll go to Taste of Chicago, okay?" a *Chicago Sun-Times* columnist wrote, referring to a local food festival. "You're an idiot," rejoined an angry reader who signed herself "a size 6 who hates Neanderthal men like you." The ad "really hit a nerve," said a spokeswoman for Ogilvy & Mather, the agency that recruited nonprofessional models whose 6-to-12 size range was below the average American woman's 14. Said college student and proud Dove girl Stacy Nadeau (far right), 21: "It's okay to be curvy and real."

THE GATES Some days in the Park, with Christo

W. MARK FELT

Deep Throat, Watergate's mystery man, finally lets his voice be heard

Deep Throat—the confidential source who helped tie the Nixon White House to Watergate—was revealed to be W. Mark Felt. Who? A career FBI agent, Felt, now 92, had told only his family about his secret identity, but when his grown children persuaded him to take credit for his actions, he went public. How will history regard him? Pundit Pat Buchanan, a former Nixon aide, called the tipster "a snitch." But Felt's grandson Nick Jones, 23, said, "[He] went well above and beyond the call of duty . . . to save his country from a horrible injustice. We all sincerely hope the country will see him this way as well."

Sometimes the gap between an artist's vision and a finished work is no more than the time it takes paint to dry. For married artists Christo and Jeanne-Claude, it was a bit longer: 26 years. The pair dreamed up *The Gates*—7,500 16-ft., vinyl-framed gates draped with tangerine-colored fabric that snaked along 23 miles of New York City's Central Park—in 1979, but red tape and fund-raising slowed its debut. In the end the couple spent no public money, financing the $21 million project through the sale of Christo's artwork. Although it was estimated that more than 4 million visitors flocked to the exhibit, some were puzzled by the meaning of all that drapery. Jeanne-Claude's enigmatic advice: "Walk under the gates," she said, "and hear them and feel them."

1

TOM & KATIE BY THE NUMBERS

On the trail of the TomKat, an exuberant creature with an exotic mating ritual

1. Often spotted in red-carpeted terrain—here it displays its trademark dip-and-smooch maneuver at the New York premiere of *War of the Worlds*—the TomKat combines the fierce hugging power of a bear with the gracefulness of a stork. (Note: If you happen upon the TomKat, please don't be afraid to take

photographs; it does not get spooked by clicking and flashing.)
2. The TomKat often bares its teeth when in a state of amorous euphoria.
3. Known for its affinity for roosting, the TomKat keeps a close eye on its offspring (here, a newly pregnant TomKat observes younglings at play in L.A.)

4. Never, ever try to domesticate the TomKat. As Oprah Winfrey discovered, it can wreak havoc on your furniture.
5. Behold the quintessential TomKat nuzzle: Notice the gentle neck-pawing and the cheek-burrowing beak.
6. The TomKat can travel at high speeds (especially during feeding time at the Ivy).

LOSING HOPE

A teen disappears on an island paradise

Natalee Holloway, 18, went to Aruba for her high school senior trip--and never returned. She was last seen in the wee hours of May 30, climbing into a car outside a Carlos 'n Charlie's restaurant with three local men. At first Joran van der Sloot, 18, told police that he and his friends, brothers Satish and Deepak Kalpoe, 18 and 21 respectively, had dropped Holloway at her hotel half an hour after leaving the restaurant. Later he changed the story, claiming he had last seen her, alive, on a beach. Natalee's mother, Beth Twitty, led an impassioned campaign to find the truth--so far to no avail. After months of investigation, Aruban police have filed no charges.

Beth Twitty (in Aruba in June) helped galvanize a massive search for her daughter and raised more than $1 million for the effort, with contributions from supporters including Courteney Cox and Sting.

HANG ON, SNUPPY

Give that dog a clone: The world's first duplicate canine

When scientists in South Korea announced the birth of Snuppy, the world's first cloned dog, Aug. 3, the Afghan hound must have caused Genetic Savings & Clone CEO Lou Hawthorne to lick his chops. After his Sausalito, Calif., company cloned a kitten from a deceased 17-year-old cat for a Texas woman—who paid $50,000 for the duplicate pet in 2004—Hawthorne envisioned an even more lucrative future for canine cloning: "The market for dogs will be enormous," he said.

JENNIFER WILBANKS

A wedding belle trades her ring for the road

Even as she continued to plan her 500-guest wedding in Duluth, Ga., Jennifer Wilbanks was plotting her escape. On April 26 she made her move: Telling her fiancé, John Mason, that she was going for a five-mile jog, Wilbanks instead faked her own kidnapping and fled, by bus, to Albuquerque. Four days later—with only 17 hours to go before her wedding—the Runaway Bride finally phoned home and, after some initial dissembling about what really happened, fessed up. Amazingly, Mason was eager to go ahead with the marriage (the two have yet to reschedule the nuptials). The police, on the other hand, weren't so forgiving—they charged Wilbanks with a felony for her deception. She pleaded no contest in June.

MISSING

CASE SOLVED: COLD FEET

Jennifer Carol Wilbanks
32 5'8" 123lbs
Brown hair / Brown eyes

770-47

THE PIANO MAN

For Britain's mute and anguished mystery man, music proved a saving grace

For months the man—tall, blond and clearly disturbed—didn't utter a word. Discovered wandering in a daze, with no identification and soaking wet on a rainless April day on England's Isle of Sheppey, he was, said Michael Camp, a social worker at Little Brook Hospital in Dartford, the most "traumatized" patient he had treated in 20 years. But after drawing a picture of a piano, the man was led to one in the hospital chapel, where he played classical and Beatles tunes with flair. "When he plays," said the hospital's chaplain, "he loses his terrified expression." Breaking his silence in August, the man was identified as Andreas Grassl, 20, a farmer's son from Bavaria who suffered from mental illness and reportedly told his family he remembered catching a ferry to Britain and a train to the Isle of Sheppey. The rest remained a mystery.

HEY JUDE, YOU MADE IT BAD

Jude Law's passion on a pool table with the nanny KO'd—for now—his wedding to Sienna Miller

In January, when it was announced that Jude Law, 33, had proposed to her on Christmas Day, girlfriend Sienna Miller declared herself "the happiest girl alive" and said, "I want a big church wedding. We haven't set a date yet, but I'm ecstatic." Even Law's not-quite-yet ex-wife, Sadie Frost (their divorce was made official in June), felt the joy. "I'm delighted for Jude and Sienna," she said.

The bliss ended abruptly in July, when Daisy Wright, 26, who worked as a nanny to Frost and Law's three children, told a London tabloid that she had trysted with Law the previous spring in New Orleans, hours after Miller, 24, who had been visiting her fiancé on the set of *All the King's Men,* left town.

Even after the couple reportedly ended their engagement, oddsmakers were left to ponder conflicting assessments of the relationship: Law and Sienna were spotted together in Paris in October, then in London a month later. "Their relationship is over," said one source. Not so, said another: "They are equally smitten."

MIND OF A KILLER

In gruesome detail—and with a chilling lack of emotion—Wichita's BTK strangler Dennis Rader, 60, described in court the crimes that terrorized his community for more than 30 years

O f victims Joseph, Julie, Josephine and Joey Otero in 1974: "I didn't have a mask on or anything. They'd already ID'd me. And I made the decision to go ahead and put them down, I guess, or strangle them. . . . I had never strangled anyone before, so I really don't know how much pressure you had to put on a person. . . . I strangled Mrs. Otero . . . then I strangled Josephine . . . and then I went over and put a bag on Junior's head."

Of victim Nancy Fox, 1977: "I dropped by once to check the mailbox to see what her name was. I found out where she worked. [After I knocked] nobody answered the door, so I went around to the back of the house, cut the phone lines. . . . I broke in and waited for her to come home in the kitchen."

Of victim Marine Hedge, 1985: "Since she lived down the street from me, I could watch [her] coming and going quite easily. . . . We walked by and waved. She liked to work in her yard as well as I like to work. . . . It was just a neighborly thing. . . . I manually strangled her when she started to scream."

Of victim Vicki Wegerle, 1986: "I used a ruse as a telephone repairman to get into her house. . . . I drew a pistol at her and asked her if she would go back to the bedroom with me. . . . She was very upset. . . . We fought quite a bit, back and forth. . . . I finally gained on her and put her down."

Of victim Dolores Davis, 1991: "I really couldn't figure out how to get in [her house], so I finally just selected a concrete block and threw it through the glass plate window. [After strangling her and putting her in the trunk of her car] I realized I had lost one of my guns. . . . I went back into the house . . . and I found it right there, so that solved that problem."

In August, Rader (right), known as the BTK killer for his self-described M.O. "Bind, Torture, Kill," was sentenced to 10 consecutive life terms for murder. "They say time heals all wounds," said Charlie Otero, 47, most of whose family were murdered by Rader. "That's a crock."

The Schiavo case struck a chord with both pro-life and right-to-die protesters.

TERRI SCHIAVO

Her life-and-death tragedy sparked a fierce national debate

Fifteen years after Michael Schiavo found his wife, Terri, unconscious on the floor of their Florida home—she had suffered cardiac arrest, and lack of oxygen had caused severe brain damage—the fight over whether to prolong her life came to its excruciating conclusion. On March 18 an earlier Florida court ruling allowed Michael to have his wife's feeding tube removed for the third time in four years. Congress intervened at the behest of Terri's parents, Robert and Mary Schindler, and asked a federal court to review the case. The Schindlers argued that Terri's brain was still functioning; Michael insisted Terri, 41, would not have wanted to exist in such a way. Even staffers at Terri's hospice got caught in the crossfire. "A lot of people have agreed to disagree, so we're not arguing in the break room anymore," said one worker. Ultimately the courts sided with Michael, refusing to order the tube reinstated. Terri died on March 31.

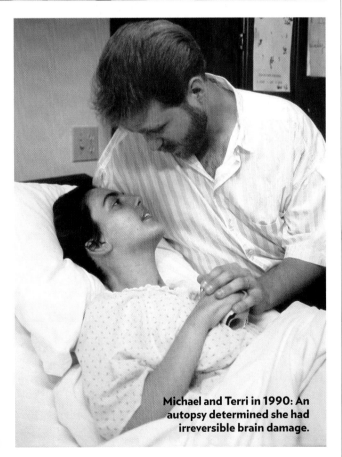

Michael and Terri in 1990: An autopsy determined she had irreversible brain damage.

PAKISTAN QUAKE

An epic disaster levels homes and leaves towns and cities in ruins in a region plagued by war and calamities

The enormous tremor—7.6 on the Richter scale—struck as schoolchildren sat in morning classes Oct. 8. Among the staggering number of victims—the death toll soared to about 80,000 in the towns and villages of northern Pakistan, India and Kashmir—were thousands of young students, crushed as buildings crumbled around them. There were miraculous tales of survival as volunteers tunneled through tons of rubble to rescue survivors trapped for days and even weeks in collapsed buildings. Hampered by rugged terrain, hostilities between neighboring Pakistan and India, thinly stretched American and allied military forces and what humanitarian groups called "donor fatigue" among organizations and individuals exhausted by the Asian tsunami and other disasters, relief efforts have in many places been stymied, leaving an estimated 2 million homeless quake victims facing a long and brutal Himalayan winter. As cold weather closed in, Jan Egeland, the U.N.'s emergency-relief coordinator, said, "We are losing the race against the clock in the small villages."

England, said her sister, "will miss [her son's] first steps" while in prison.

SCOTT PETERSON

AN UGLY ACT OF WAR

21 months after the scandal broke, Lynndie England, the soldier made notorious by the Abu Ghraib prison-abuse photos, goes to jail herself

Even Lynndie England seemed to find it hard to look as the photos of prisoner abuse at Iraq's Abu Ghraib prison were projected on a 12-ft. screen in a Fort Hood, Texas, courtroom: a group of naked Iraqi men stacked in a pile, a hooded naked detainee, and England herself holding another naked Iraqi on a leash. "She's very sorry," said her sister Jessica Klinestiver. "She didn't want to do any of that."

But she did. In her defense, England's lawyers claimed she was manipulated by ex-boyfriend and fellow Abu Ghraib guard Charles Graner, who was already serving 10 years at Leavenworth for his part in the abuse. (Graner, who denied he is the father of England's young son, wed another Abu Ghraib reservist, Megan Ambuhl, in April.)

On Sept. 27 England, 22, was sentenced to three years in prison. Her sister insisted she was following orders: "She was told by superiors to pose in the pictures." But England herself told the court, "I could have said no."

JUSTICE FOR LACI AND LORI

Two cases, two killers, same result: a new life in jail—or worse

MARK HACKING

In headline-making murder cases, it was a good year for justice: Two notorious killers were given new addresses and radically simplified wardrobes. Most prominently, Scott Peterson (left) moved into a San Quentin cell in the spring, following his November 2004 conviction for the murder of his pregnant wife, Laci, and their unborn child. While some inmates in the mid-19th-century prison enjoy a view of the San Francisco Bay, where Peterson dumped his wife's body, he can't see much of anything from his 41-sq.-ft. space on death row. While appealing his sentence, a process that may forestall his execution for 20 years or more, he bided his time by decorating his cell with photos of Laci (including one in her wedding dress); visiting with his parents, who make the 1,000-mile round-trip drive from San Diego about once a week; and reading as many as 80 or more letters he receives each week. Many are from female fans, like the one who dubbed him Scottie-Too-Hottie.

"Scott's keeping his spirits pretty high," said a friend of the family. "He has the attitude that he didn't do anything wrong, and he's waiting for the day when he can come out and do his ha-ha dance and tell the world, 'See, I didn't do it.'"

While Peterson, 32, still maintains he was wrongly convicted, another infamous killer of his pregnant spouse, Mark Hacking (right), 29, forsook all claims of innocence in a plea bargain that allowed him to avoid trial—and a possible death sentence. "I intentionally shot Lori Hacking in the head with a .22 rifle on July 19, 2004," he confessed. "I'm tormented every waking minute by what I did. I can't explain why I did it."

Prosecutors could. They said he killed his wife after she discovered that Hacking, a doctor's son whose ambitions to become a doctor himself were frustrated when he flunked out of college, had lied about being admitted to medical school. Sentenced to six years to life at Utah State Prison in Draper, Hacking, 29, would likely serve 25 to 35 years, his lawyer estimated. Still, the victim's mother, Eraldo Soares, found little comfort, exclaiming after the sentencing, "How could Mark do that to my daughter!"

TOASTS ON THE TOWN

Jamie Foxx didn't let his Oscar win or his *Miami Vice* shooting schedule mess up his pace-setting nightlife

After scoring his Best Actor Oscar in March, Jamie Foxx made a solemn vow: to party the night away. It was a promise he kept on keeping. After being toasted by all of Hollywood for his *Ray* win, Foxx, 38, jetted to Florida, where he and *Miami Vice* costar Colin Farrell spent the next months letting the good times roll. And roll. Celebrating Farrell's 29th birthday on May 31, the two quaffed Remy Martin and chatted up available women. On June 24 they party-hopped till dawn, ending up at Mansion, where Foxx no doubt discussed quantum theory with available women. The next night he hit up Privé, sans Farrell, and stood on the bar, pouring shots into the mouths of available women. "I always tell him, 'Stay focused on the work,'" said *Ray* director Taylor Hackford. Somehow Foxx did, finding time to wrap *Vice,* costar in *Jarhead* and record his first major label album, *Unpredictable.*

FACE UP TO METH

Meth users unintentionally star in a dramatic antidrug campaign

Like crack cocaine in the '80s, say experts, crystal methamphetamine is cheap, potent, alarmingly addictive and well on its way to becoming a law enforcement and public health crisis of epidemic proportions. It causes severe brain damage, as demonstrated by an X-ray that revealed actual holes in one user's brain tissue. "I got sick at my stomach" upon seeing such evidence said Arab, Ala., obstetrician Dr. Mary Holley, who founded Mothers Against Methamphetamine to warn of the drug's dangers. Police in Portland, Ore., took a different tack, distributing photos (including those below) as dramatic evidence of meth's ruinous effects.

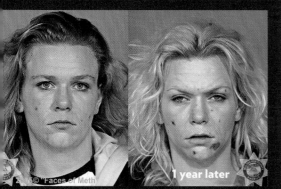

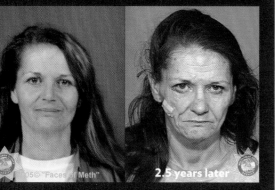

I. LEWIS 'SCOOTER' LIBBY

A White House scandal puts Vice President Cheney's right-hand man in the hot seat

After two years of investigating who was responsible for leaking the identity of CIA agent Valerie Plame (wife of vociferous White House critic Joseph Wilson), special prosecutor Patrick Fitzgerald ultimately indicted I. Lewis "Scooter" Libby. As Chief of Staff to Vice President Dick Cheney, Libby—who resigned as soon as the indictment was handed down—was known in Washington as "Cheney's Cheney," a hard-nosed politico who liked to keep a low profile even while wielding immense influence on the biggest issues of the day, including the war in Iraq. Charged with perjury, false statements and obstruction of justice because of his allegedly untruthful grand jury testimony, he now finds himself firmly in the scandal's spotlight. If convicted, Libby—who pleaded not guilty—could face up to 30 years in prison.

COSTUME SQUALLS

THE **Sun** HOLS FROM **£9.50**
8-PAGE PULLOUT & BOOKING FORM
LAST CHANCE TO JOIN

HARRY THE NAZI

Prince's swastika outfit at party

Madonna reveals a controversial habit; Prince Harry, partying in Nazi regalia, learns wrong from Reich

I
t was a very good year for the British tabloids. Fortune first smiled in January when bonny Prince Harry had his "Springtime for Hitler" moment, appearing at a friend's London costume party decked out like a loyal Nazi dignitary, swastika armband and all. "Shameful," said Rabbi Marvin Hier of the Simon Wiesenthal Center in Los Angeles, who joined a worldwide chorus of condemnation. "I am very sorry if I caused any offense; it was a poor choice of costume," said the pub-loving Prince of Understatement. Also misplacing their sensitivity chips were Madonna, who attended a Purim party at London's Kabbalah Centre in March dressed as a nun, and hubby Guy Ritchie, who went as the Pope. As the real pontiff was in worsening health at the time, Catholic League president Bill Donohue decreed that the costumes "crossed the line from bad taste to obscenity." Madonna and hubby "meant no disrespect at all," said her publicist, adding that Madonna had said jokingly that her Catholic father might "finally be proud of me."

Guy Ritchie, Madonna and Prince Harry caught flak for outrageous outfits.

TUXEDO JUNCTION

Cold, cold comfort: A film about the familial devotion of emperor penguins becomes the year's sleeper hit

You might not expect a graphic French film about the sex lives of naked bipeds to have great appeal for certain segments of the public. But conservatives and liberals alike flocked to filmmaker Luc Jacquet's *March of the Penguins*. The uplifting wildlife documentary chronicles the mating habits of emperor penguins, who pair off in monogamous couples and trek 70 miles to their Antarctic breeding ground in temperatures that can sink to 150 degrees below zero. Exquisitely shot by Jacquet and two fellow Frenchmen who spent 13 months living among the foul-weather fowl, the surprise hit starred some surprisingly big hams. "They liked to put themselves in front of the lens," codirector Jerome Maison said of two bold penguins, "sometimes to the point that we weren't able to film the others."

FEELING BETTER

She overcomes a harrowing bout of postpartum depression —and Tom Cruise's criticism. Now Brooke Shields says she's expecting again

An icon of beauty for four decades, Brooke Shields published *Down Came the Rain,* a frank chronicle of her battle with severe postpartum depression following the birth of her daughter Rowan Francis in 2003. Plagued by suicidal thoughts and an urge to harm her baby, Shields got help through therapy and the antidepressant Paxil. "As time passed," she wrote, "I was beginning to feel more and more what I thought a mother would feel."

Later Tom Cruise, a devoted Scientologist, publicly criticized her for relying on drugs rather than diet and exercise. Shields responded with an op-ed in *The New York Times,* and other sufferers rallied to her defense. "When Tom becomes a woman and has a baby and has postpartum," said Marie Osmond, "then he can become an expert." For Shields, 40, and husband Chris Henchy, 41, there was a sweet coda: Their second child is due in 2006.

PARIS HILTON

Through all the bling and arrows brought on by her outrageous fortune, she basks in the viewfinder

For Paris Hilton it was a year of ups (Engaged to Greek billionaire Paris Latsis! Another season of her reality TV show *The Simple Life*! The cover of *Vanity Fair*!), downs (The engagement's off! The show's canceled!) and never-ending gossip (Somebody hacked her T-Mobile Sidekick II! She's dating another Greek billionaire! She's feuding with Nicole Richie! And while we're at it: Where in the world is Tinkerbell, her once ubiquitous Chihuahua?).

No matter. Paris (at right, in Cannes) soldiered on, persevering through thin and thin, focused— resolute, unstoppable—on her one true love: the nearest lens.

HOLLYWOOD &CRIME

The year in celebrity justice—
from Russell Crowe's phone rage
to Michael Jackson's 'Not guilty'

Surprisingly upbeat as his child-molestation trial loomed in January, Michael Jackson at first appeared not to take seriously charges that he had plied his then-13-year-old accuser with wine and porn and groped him during sleepovers at Neverland ranch. "He's still in his own Neverland," said a family friend.

By trial's end, 14 weeks and more than 140 witnesses later, Jackson had grown increasingly gaunt and weak, the result, a friend told PEOPLE, of his having subsisted for months on little more than a liquid diet and sedatives. Facing 20 years in prison if convicted on all 10 criminal counts, Jackson, 46, reacted as if in a trance when the verdict was finally read June 13: not guilty on all counts. Jurors later said they agreed with the defense that, as one said, "the accuser's mother was an opportunist." Added another: "Everybody thought she was not truthful."

Whisked from the Santa Maria, Calif., courthouse, Jackson did not even pause to give his customary wave to the hundreds of cheering fans gathered at the gates of Neverland. Later, his father, Joe, explained that rather than celebrating, Jackson was "in bed right now. He's trying to get rest, to get back strong."

Jackson sequestered himself at Neverland in the weeks after the trial, then flew with his three children to the Persian Gulf Kingdom of Bahrain, where he relaxed as a guest of Sheik Abdullah. "He needs to rest," a friend said of the singer, "and then think about a comeback."

I never saw or heard anything to suggest that he was a pedophile," Macaulay Culkin's father, Kit, said after his son testified for the defense.

MARTHA STEWART

On Aug. 31 she dumped her least favorite accessory: an ankle bracelet

At 12:30 a.m. on Fri., March 4, Martha Stewart left Alderson Federal Prison Camp with the weight of the world—except for a now-famous gray poncho knit by a fellow inmate—lifted from her shoulders. "I'm dreaming of cappuccino . . . [and] I really missed lemons," said the überhomemaker after finishing her five-month sentence for charges including conspiracy and obstruction of justice and returning to her Bedford, N.Y., estate.

Stewart, 64, still had one big payment left on her debt to society: five months of home confinement. Even though home was a 153-acre horse farm, the multitasking corporate exec found the sentence to be a pain in the ankle: The monitoring device she wore caused her physical distress, she said, and she also chafed at trying to cram her hectic schedule into the 48 hours per week she was granted in the outside world (and used to help revitalize her company and start two TV shows). "You have to watch the clock constantly because you're only allowed out of your home for a limited period, and for a busy person, watching the clock, and knowing other people are watching the clock, is extremely difficult," she said.

In the end Stewart's clock-watching skills were, apparently, imperfect: Authorities added three weeks to her house arrest for violating the terms of her confinement.

More than 7,500 ponchos (like the one Stewart showed off at her first post-hoosegow press conference) were sold for charity within 48 hours.

COURT DRAMA

Robert Blake faces trial for the murder of his wife, Bonny

"The cause of this whole ordeal," Robert Blake's son Noah said near the end of his father's criminal trial for the murder of his wife, Bonny Lee Bakley, "was my father's choice to be around Bonny. What's sad is that he didn't feel good enough about himself to be around better people." A 44-year-old grifter and alleged con artist whom Blake, 72, married in 2000, Bakley was shot and killed near a favorite L.A. restaurant in 2001. Facing life in prison, Blake, the former "Our Gang" comedies child actor and star of TV's *Baretta*, claimed innocence. Confronting his father after the murder, Noah asked, " 'Did you have anything to do with this?' He looked me in the eyes and said, 'Absolutely not.' I never needed to ask him again." Acquitted March 16 by jurors, some of whom said they found the circumstantial evidence against him "flimsy," Blake wasn't so lucky Nov. 18, when he was found liable for the wrongful death of his wife in a civil suit brought by her family. He was ordered to pay $30 million in damages.

"He wasn't always a tough guy," son Noah said of Blake (on trial in September 2004).

RICHARD HATCH

IRS says *Survivor* ace skipped taxes

While he was in the process of outwitting, outlasting and outplaying his fellow castaways to become the first *Survivor* champ, Richard Hatch proved he could be one cocky contender. "I've got the million-dollar check written in my name," he declared in the very first episode of the CBS reality series. He turned out to be right, of course—but it's the game of real life that he may have played imperfectly. On Sept. 8, Hatch, 44, was indicted in Providence, R.I., for failing to pay taxes. Prosecutors allege that between 2000 and 2001 he neglected to report $1.4 million in income—including his 1 million *Survivor* smackers—and that he pocketed $36,500 that had been donated to a nonprofit camp he runs for troubled kids. Hatch, who faces up to 10 years in prison and a $500,000 fine, said he was "absolutely not guilty," claiming he thought CBS was responsible for footing the IRS tab. Unfortunately, the possibility of him winning immunity seems out of the question.

KATE MOSS
Supermodel's nose caught in an unflattering pose

It could have been a great year for Kate Moss. She made history with her 10th British *Vogue* cover. Retailer H&M named her the face of Stella McCartney's new line. She was still one of the brightest lights on the fashion runways. But on Sept. 15 Britain's *Daily Mirror* ran front-page photos of her apparently snorting cocaine, leading many high-end clients—including H&M, jeweler H. Stern and Chanel—to drop the waif supermodel. Moss, 31, never admitted to using drugs but did issue a carefully worded apology, reading in part, "I accept that there are various personal issues I need to address." She later checked herself into an Arizona rehab facility. London police are investigating Moss's actions, though some legal experts say an arrest is unlikely unless there is proof the substance in the photos was indeed cocaine.

A RAPPER RHYMES WHILE DOING TIME

Lil' Kim faces the music for lying about a shoot-out

No matter how big a rapper's gift for rhyme or how large her vaults of bling, she's nothing without street cred. Lil' Kim, 31, scored an armored car's worth Sept. 19 when she began serving a 366-day sentence for perjury. A week later her fourth album, *The Naked Truth*, completed along with three videos during her last days of freedom, was released. According to press reports, she's already hard at work in her Philadelphia cell writing new songs for a follow-up. Before beginning her sentence, Kim, née Kimberly Jones, who was convicted for lying to a grand jury about a 2001 shooting involving her manager and a longtime friend, said she planned to catch up on her reading. As for the judge who sentenced her to a year and a day, he "wasn't half as mean as he wanted to be," she told PEOPLE. "The unknown makes you nervous, but . . . there's no reason for me to be scared."

DAILY Mirror — EXCLUSIVE — THESE AMAZING PHOTOS INSIDE

COCAINE KATE
Supermodel Kate Moss snorts line after line

RUSSELL CROWE

After having his buttons pushed by a faulty hotel
phone, the moody actor dials up an assault charge

R are's the year that Russell Crowe's temper doesn't make headline writers happy. 2005 was no exception: At about 4 a.m. on June 6, Crowe,
41, tried to call his wife in Australia from his $3,000-a-night suite at
the Mercer Hotel in New York City. Unable to get his call through, and very
unsatisfied by a desk clerk's response to his dilemma, Crowe unplugged the
offending phone, headed to the front desk and threw it at employee Nestor
Estrada, inflicting a one-inch cut on the victim's cheek. Crowe was charged
with second-degree assault and criminal possession of a weapon (the
phone). After fessing up to his misdeed, he eventually reached a financial
settlement—reportedly in the low six figures—with Estrada, and escaped jail
time after pleading guilty to third-degree assault Nov. 18.

You're married! The mogul and his fiancée say 'I do' at a Mar-a-Lago wedding of typically Trumpian splendor

DONALD & MELANIA

No, *of course* it wasn't simple. Forty-five chefs, 100 limo drivers, 10,000 white flowers (hauled from New York) and approximately 450 guests—from Hillary Clinton to P. Diddy—were on hand when Donald Trump wed his fiancée in Palm Beach on Jan. 22. Shortly after 7 p.m., as a soloist sang "Ave Maria," Melania Knauss, 34, entered the Episcopal Church of Bethesda-by-the-Sea. She briefly faltered en route to the altar, and understandably so: Her Christian Dior gown weighed a whopping 60 lbs. and had a 13-ft. train and a 16-ft. veil. "I didn't practice walking with the dress," she confessed. But moments later, "I just saw Donald's happy face," she said, "and everything happened like, fast, wow." Guests agreed. "It was quick but beautiful and perfect," said *American Idol*'s Simon Cowell (who noted that the soloist

"People told me they felt love and elegance and grace," says Melania of the ceremony.

The Dior gown, which had 300 ft. of white satin, took 28 seamstresses 1,000-plus hours to make. The cost: over $100,000.

> ' WE COMPLETELY FORGOT EVERYTHING AROUND US.
> IT WAS JUST US TWO. IT WAS BEAUTIFUL' -MELANIA

The pastry chef spent two months creating nearly 3,000 roses from icing for the 5-ft., 200-lb. Grand Marnier chiffon cake.

Trump spent $45 million building the Mar-a-Lago ballroom that served as the reception hall.

THE RING
Melania's Graff engagement ring is nearly 12 carats. A rep for the jeweler calls it "a million-dollar stone."

did miss one note). "I give it a nine."

At the reception, held at Mar-a-Lago, a private resort owned by the twice-divorced Trump, 58, guests chatted over caviar, lobster and truffle appetizers. At around 10 p.m. the Trumps had their first dance, to Puccini's "Nessun Dorma." Says Melania: "We completely forgot everything around us." Leading the toasts, Trump's son Eric welcomed her to the family, saying, "I know this is the last time I'll ever have to stand up here." Added The Donald: "Melania and I have been together for six years. They've been the best six years of my life in every way." Melania slipped out about 1 a.m. to change into a lightweight Vera Wang dress, making it easier, as she said, to "party all night!"

Trump finally carried her over the threshold of their suite at 4 a.m. "Donald has always said he used to make a bad husband and a great father," says his pal Pat O'Brien. "This time around he wants to make a great father and a great husband." He'll soon have the chance: The couple are expecting their first child in March.

BEN AFFLECK & JENNIFER GARNER

The Sturm und Drang behind, Affleck takes the fast track to the altar—with a different Jennifer

On the heels of the media frenzy that was Bennifer (a.k.a. Ben Affleck and Jennifer Lopez), Affleck's courtship of Jennifer Garner was so low-key that even after the *Alias* star began sporting a diamond bauble on her left hand 10 months into their courtship, the pair still declined to acknowledge an engagement. Confirmation came only in the wake of the couple's June 29 wedding, reportedly at Bruce Willis's home in the Turks and Caicos Islands. Guests included Garner's *Alias* dad, Victor Garber, but neither her real parents nor Affleck's (or even Willis, for that matter). Unlike the $2 million extravaganza planned for the J.Lo nuptials, this affair was free of bling and excess, the most noteworthy detail the obvious swell of Garner's once-supertaut belly—a pregnancy that Garner, 33, and Affleck, 32, confirmed post-vows at the same time they confirmed their marriage. With a baby girl born on Dec. 1, the couple slipped into parenthood with a minimum of fuss—and seemingly a maximum of pleasure in one another's company.

TIFFANI THIESSEN & BRADY SMITH

They're all grown up: *90210*ers reunite at a costar's nuptials

The wedding had the feel of a reunion when Tori Spelling, Jason Priestley and other *Beverly Hills, 90210* alums turned up at a private estate in Montecito, Calif., on July 9 to see their former costar Tiffani Thiessen tie the knot with actor Brady Smith. As Thiessen stood by Smith's side during the early-evening garden ceremony, their pastor offered a tip for a long, happy marriage: one 30-second hug and one 10-second kiss per day—starting immediately. When the pastor got to "You may kiss the bride," the 135 guests began counting to 10. The infectious joy continued well into the evening at Santa Barbara's Hotel Andalucia, where Thiessen, 31, and Smith, 33, spent their first married night—and awoke to day two of the 10-second rule.

MARY KAY LETOURNEAU & VILI FUALAAU

After she did seven-plus years for child rape, the ex-teacher and her former sixth-grade pet made it legal

Mary Kay Letourneau had waited more than seven years behind bars to marry the boy-turned-man of her dreams, so what was another two hours? That's how tardy the 43-year-old was for her May 20 wedding to Vili Fualaau, 21, the former pupil she first bedded when he was 12—an affair that produced two children and sent her to the slammer. Finally she glided down the aisle before 225 guests at the Columbia Winery in Woodinville, Wash. "Where you stay, I will stay, and where you die, I will die," said Mary Kay, according to *Entertainment Tonight* and *The Insider*, which taped the event. Vili promised, "From the beginning till eternity ends, to love, honor and respect every aspect of your journey." "She weathered her time, and they're in love," said friend Robert Eldridge. "Who are we to argue?"

SANDRA BULLOCK & JESSE JAMES

She thought she'd never marry—until she met a guy as low-key as she is famously friendly

The invitation advertised a July 16 barbeque to celebrate Sandra Bullock's 41st birthday. But as 270 guests sipped cocktails, the lights dimmed for a short video featuring the couple talking cute about each other. The clip ended with an announcement by Jesse James, 36, the star of Discovery Channel's *Monster Garage* vehicle-makeover show, and Bullock's main squeeze since 2004: "We've been engaged since October, suckers!" Bagpipers led the delighted suckers to a grove on the Solvang, Calif., estate. Laughter gave way to tears when Bullock appeared in white—cowboy boots peeking from beneath her gown—on the arm of her dad and the recorded sounds of an aria sung by her mom, Helga, an opera singer who died of cancer in 2000, filled the air. Later, Bullock's choice of music for the first dance said it all: a remix of the Motown classic "Best Thing That Ever Happened to Me."

HEIDI KLUM & SEAL

Where does a British pop star marry the German model with whom he shares a California address? Mexico

To ensure that their ceremony would be paparazzi-free, German supermodel Heidi Klum, 31, and British pop-star Seal, 42, exchanged vows in front of a single person: their nondenominational officiant. By the time their 40 guests arrived at the beachside canopy on Seal's cliffside estate in Costa Careyes, Mexico, the five-months-pregnant Klum and Seal were already wed. Still, there was plenty to savor during the May 10 celebration. Klum was a knockout in a Vera Wang gown—as was her daughter Leni, 1, who wore an identical gown. Pachelbel's *Canon in D* was offered on a Stradivarius. When guests repaired to Seal's home for the reception, they found a cake topped with miniatures of Seal and Klum. The wedding, Klum explained, was never meant to be "Donald Trump style. That's not us." Which isn't to say the couple do not have their own exotic panache. Seal, who started dating Klum while she was pregnant with Leni (whose biological father is Italian businessman Flavio Briatore, 55, from whom Klum split in February 2004), proposed to Klum that December in a specially built igloo atop a 14,000-ft. glacier. And to make room for their burgeoning brood—son Henry was born in September—the pair recently snapped up a $4.3 million Bel Air estate. The result? Familial bliss. "I would die if I didn't have my music," said Seal. "But I love my family much more."

CHARLES & CAMILLA

With his sons' good wishes,
the Prince and his longtime
love finally make it to the altar

So what if the groom never publicly kissed the bride? Where do you think they were—France? Anyway, *behind* the scenes, Camilla Parker Bowles caught some even more significant smooches. As she and Prince Charles left their Windsor Castle reception April 9, a beaming Prince Harry pecked his new stepmum on both cheeks. Prince William followed suit; then the brothers showered the newlyweds with confetti. All this from lads theretofore never even photographed beside Camilla. As Harry said later, "William and I love her to bits."

Certainly the high spirits made up for a Queen who barely cracked a public smile and skipped the civil ceremony at

After the civil ceremony, said Camilla's friend William Shawcross, "William and Harry were milling around the crowd, extremely cheerful."

"SHE SAID, "DON'T YOU DARE. WE DON'T DO THAT IN BRITAIN""

—WEDDING GUEST JOAN RIVERS, AFTER OFFERING TO THROW CAMILLA A LINGERIE SHOWER

30   68

Windsor's town hall. For that, Charles, 56, and Camilla, 57, arrived to a cheering crowd of 20,000—modest compared to the millions who thronged London's streets for Charles's first wedding. Once hitched, they secured a blessing from the Archbishop of Canterbury, then went on to the tea-and-finger-food reception, joining the Queen and approximately 750 guests, including Prime Minister Tony Blair, Phil Collins and Joan Rivers, who offered to throw Camilla a lingerie shower. "She said, 'Don't you dare,'" Rivers reported. "'We don't do that in Britain.'"

Once persona non grata at the palace, Camilla, now Duchess of Cornwall, is the senior female royal after Elizabeth II. A *Sunday Times* poll showed 73 percent of Brits don't want her to be queen. Not that it mattered to the couple. Said pal Jilly Cooper: "You could have warmed your hands on their happiness."

Heading off in the Bentley that Charles's sons decorated, the newlyweds honeymooned in Scotland.

ROB MARIANO & AMBER BRKICH

On a beach, reality TV's royal couple formed an eternal alliance

Amber Brkich always dreamed of a beach wedding. But no girlhood fantasy could have conjured up the Paradise Island nuptials she shared on April 16 with Rob Mariano, 230 guests—and a swarm of TV camera-crew members, there to film a CBS special that would air a month later. As the sweetheart winners of *Survivor: All-Stars,* Brkich, 26, a former health-club employee, and Mariano, 29, an ex-construction worker, had announced their engagement in May 2004 on the *All-Stars* finale. With nearly a year—and a lavish CBS budget—to make plans, no detail was over-looked. Invitations went out in glass bottles filled with sand and tiny seashells. The extensive cast included 8 bridesmaids, 11 groomsmen and a 50-member gospel choir. But beneath a seashell-covered canopy, the moment was theirs, alone, when Rob told Amber, "I've never met anyone who's made me feel so special."

DEMI MOORE & ASHTON KUTCHER

One for the ages: Moore and Kutcher tie the knot, Kabbalah style

For two years their famously May-September romance (she's 42; he's 27) sparked plenty of are-they-for-real skepticism. On Sept. 24 Demi Moore and Ashton Kutcher proved naysayers wrong: The couple wed in a Kabbalah-inspired ceremony at their Beverly Hills home. Standing under a chuppah, or Jewish marriage canopy, the bride and groom repeated blessings led by a rabbi. And contrary to rumor, the wedding was not Kutcher's most elaborate *Punk'd* prank to date. They exchanged vows before 100 guests, including Moore's ex Bruce Willis and their daughters Rumer, 17, Scout, 14, and Tallulah, 11, who refer to Kutcher as "MOD," or "My Other Dad." "The girls gave beautiful tributes," says a guest. "It was just down-to-earth."

VINCE NEIL & LIA GERARDINI

The only wedding with M.C. Hammer, Mötley Crüe, *The Surreal Life*—and love

Oddly, there were no klieg lights or onstage explosions, but there *were* waterworks. "Everybody was crying," said Mötley Crüe frontman Vince Neil, 43, of his Jan. 9 marriage to Lia Gerardini, 37. "I started crying, Tommy Lee started crying, then everyone just lost it. It was very sentimental, very heartfelt." The wedding—the fourth for Neil and second for Gerardini—was performed by rapper-turned-minister M.C. Hammer, Neil's castmate on the WB reality show *The Surreal Life* in 2003. For the reception, a hotel ballroom was converted into a nightclub where 150 guests lounged on leopard-skin furniture. "The wedding was like Vince and I," said Gerardini, a former plastic-surgery-center administrator who met Neil at a concert seven years ago. "Very romantic with a touch of rock and roll."

JASON PRIESTLEY & NAOMI LOWDE

The *Beverly Hills, 90210* vet opts for a more exotic zip to marry girlfriend Naomi Lowde

Sage advice for grooms-to-be: "When it comes to a woman and her wedding, you just have to let her do her thing," said Priestley, 35, who wed British makeup artist Naomi Lowde, 29, on May 14 in the Bahamas. For the bride that meant a 1940s-themed, gardenia-scented, beachside service. The couple, who met on a London street in 2000, were joined by some 120 guests, including *90210* alums Jennie Garth, Tiffani Thiessen and Tori Spelling. Reception revelers heard a live set by the rock band Barenaked Ladies (longtime Priestley pals) and dined on lobster and steak. There was even a surprise arranged by the groom—an evening fireworks display. "This brought us all together," said Priestley of the festivities. "And it's great to see."

LITTLE STARS

From Adelaide to Zahara, the newest crop of celeb babies had their parents bursting with pride (and longing for sleep!)

CARNIE WILSON
"She's really calm and sweet," the singer said of daughter Lola Sofia, born April 22. (Dad is Wilson's husband, musician Rob Bonfiglio, 38.) After struggling with postpartum depression—"You're overwhelmed with love and joy, then sadness and fear"—Wilson, 37, is savoring motherhood: "This little angel, this little Dunkin' Donut, has changed my whole life."

ANGELINA JOLIE
The 30-year-old actress adopted daughter Zahara Marley, an Ethiopian orphan, in July. After a brief health scare, she blossomed under her mom's TLC. Adoption "is a very special thing," Jolie said. "There's something about making a choice, waking up and traveling somewhere and finding your family."

SHARON STONE
"I have been trying to adopt a second child for years . . . so I didn't totally, totally believe it until he was in my arms," the actress, 47, said of bringing home son Laird, who joined his 5-year-old brother, Roan, in May. "The only thing better than one is two."

RACHEL GRIFFITHS
Why the name Adelaide, who was born on June 23 after a mere 90 minutes of labor? "I just love old-fashioned girl names," says the Aussie actress, 36. (And new-fangled ones for boys: Adelaide's big bro is Banjo.)

SEAN ASTIN
The *Lord of the Rings* star and his wife, Christine, 37, welcomed daughter Isabella Louise on July 22. (She joins big sisters Alexandra, 8, and Elizabeth, 3.) Will they add to their brood again? "My wife says we can consider adopting at some point, but the factory's closed," says Astin, 34. "But you never know."

"He looks great," said Kerrigan (with day-old Brian on April 15). "He's very content."

AT LONG LAST, A WISH FULFILLED

After eight years and six miscarriages, skater Nancy Kerrigan welcomed a second son

When skater Nancy Kerrigan welcomed 7-lb., 9-oz. son Brian on April 14, she had an especially eager helper at the ready: older son Matthew, 8, who immediately began holding the baby and "waiting for him to wake up so he could feed him," said Kerrigan. "He thinks it's the greatest thing ever. He has had this as Christmas and birthday wishes since he was 2."

The birth completed a long and painful journey for Kerrigan, 35, and her husband, Jerry Solomon, 50, President of StarGames. The 1994 Olympic silver medalist had suffered through six miscarriages over eight years before Brian's arrival. "It's like living on a roller coaster," Kerrigan said of her struggles. "You have to learn to love yourself and be happy with yourself, because it's really out of your control."

Combining her double axels with motherhood, Kerrigan is delighting in her newest addition. "It took a long time for this guy," she said of Brian, whom she delivered via C-section near the family's Lynnfield, Mass., home. "Since we had Matthew, we have been hoping this would happen." Happily, everyone got their wish.

JOAN LUNDEN
The broadcaster, 54, and her husband, Jeff Konigsberg, 44, pulled double duty with the March 1 arrival (via surrogate) of their *second* set of twins in just two years: Jack Andrew and Kimberly Elise.

PRINCE ALBERT
In July Monaco's 47-year-old sovereign acknowledged paternity of 22-month-old Alexandre, a son whom he fathered with ex-flame Nicole Coste.

MICHELLE BRANCH
"Whenever I put the Police on, she really rocks out," the singer, 22, said of daughter Owen, born Aug. 3.

LANCE
& SHERYL

On bended knee with a
black-velvet box? How
passé. This year Lance
proposed to Sheryl on a
bike trail. DJ AM gave
Nicole *two* rings. And
Garth asked for Trisha's
hand in front of 7,000
fans. After all that, how
could a girl say no?

The seven-time Tour de France champ now needs a bicycle built for two. On an Idaho mountain-biking trip in August, Armstrong, 34, bestowed a diamond ring on singer Crow, 43. Plans for a 2006 wedding kicked into high gear. "This is the sweetest, most wonderful thing," said his mom, Linda Armstrong Kelly. "Being together makes them complete."

GARTH BROOKS &
TRISHA YEARWOOD

With his longtime love at his side, Brooks unveiled a bronze statue of himself at Buck Owen's Crystal Palace before 7,000 fans in May. One problem: The statue's left hand sported a wedding band. Brooks, 43, corrected the discrepancy by dropping to one knee and proposing to a teary Yearwood, 40, who said, "What I'm feeling right now I would wish on anyone."

NICOLE RICHIE & DJ AM

In February, DJ AM (a.k.a. Adam Goldstein), 32, asked for Richie's hand with a diamond-and-pink-sapphire ring. Then he surprised Richie, 23, with another diamond bauble at their July engagement party. Although the two were scheduled to ring in the new year together, they ended their engagement in December.

MATT DAMON & LUCIANA BARROSO

Soon the actor's 9,500-sq.-ft. Miami Beach mansion will be a full house: In July Damon, 34, asked his 29-year-old girlfriend—who has a daughter, Alexia, 7—to marry him. Said the smitten actor in July: "Don't make me talk about my girlfriend, because I will start jumping on this chair."

REBECCA ROMIJN & JERRY O'CONNELL

"I've had a great year," said Romijn, 32, of her courtship with the *Crossing Jordan* star. It got even better in September, when O'Connell, 31, popped the question at his parents' Manhattan apartment. "Next up is kids," said the actor.

ROD STEWART & PENNY LANCASTER

During a March visit to the Eiffel Tower, rocker Rod Stewart, 60, dropped to one knee, whipped out a princess-cut diamond ring, and proposed to his girlfriend of 5½ years. "I was so shocked I couldn't speak for an hour afterwards," said Lancaster, 34. "It was all so perfect." In June the couple announced another surprise: They are expecting a baby in December.

Blink and you might have missed some of the year's ill-fated unions

BREAK UP!

She had him at goodbye. After just four months of marriage, Renée Zellweger filed for an annulment of her marriage to country crooner Kenny Chesney on Sept. 14. The couple's whirlwind romance had begun Jan. 15, when they met at NBC's tsunami-relief telethon. For the *Cold Mountain* Oscar winner, "it was love at first sight," said a pal. It came even earlier for Chesney: Zellweger's famous Jerry Maguire line—"You had me at hello"—had inspired his 1999 No. 1 hit ballad. Still, both strived to keep their budding romance out of the limelight. The first public inkling came on April 29, when Zellweger, 36, popped up onstage to deliver a surprise margarita and a kiss to Chesney, 37, at a concert in Jacksonville, Fla. Ten days later the couple wed in a stealth ceremony on St. John before 35 family members and close friends. A mere 128 days later, the marriage was over. Chesney said he was caught completely off guard. "I'm sad, I'm angry, and I'm hurt and confused," he told PEOPLE. Still, he and Zellweger remained on friendly terms and were united in keeping the details of what went wrong a private affair. Summed up Zellweger: "Kenny and I decided not to publicly discuss the details of our relationship because we felt that it would be a compromise of personal integrity."

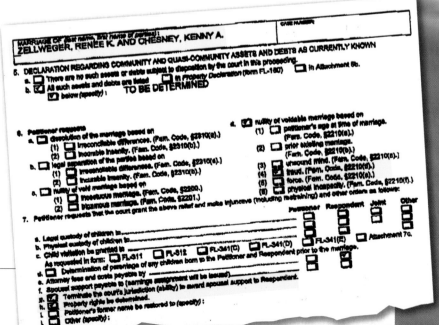

IN WRITING
In her Sept. 14 petition (left), Zellweger (with Chesney May 9) cited "fraud" as grounds for the annulment. When that term raised eyebrows, Zellweger responded that it was "simply legal language and not a reflection of Kenny's character."

TORI SPELLING & CHARLIE SHANIAN

The decline of the former *90210* star's marriage plays out like a nighttime drama

The bride's bad trip down the aisle wasn't a good sign. Before exchanging vows in July 2004 with Shanian, 35, a writer and actor, Spelling, 31—the actress daughter of TV mogul Aaron and his wife, Candy—got her heel stuck in her gown and couldn't budge. Maybe her shoe was trying to tell her something. Thirteen months later the *90210* alum moved out on Shanian, whom she'd met in L.A. in 2002. "I went into the marriage with the best intentions, hopes and dreams," Spelling told PEOPLE. "I don't know exactly what happened and when things started to go wrong." They went downhill fast in August, according to one insider. On the Ottawa set of *Mind over Murder,* a TV movie, Spelling became smitten with her married costar Dean McDermott, 38. She says the romance began after she and Shanian split up. "That's all news to Charlie," said his lawyer after Shanian filed for divorce Oct. 12. "He believed they were happily married until Sept. 19," the day he says they separated. "No one meant any harm to anyone," says a friend of Spelling's. "You can't help who you fall in love with."

McDermott (with Spelling in October) split from his wife a month earlier.

THE GROOVE IS GONE

After a startling discovery, Terry McMillan jettisons the young lover who inspired *How Stella Got Her Groove Back*

Readers and moviegoers who cheered Terry McMillan's *How Stella Got Her Groove Back,* the 1996 bestselling book and 1998 hit film based on her love affair with Jamaican dreamboat Jonathan Plummer, were dismayed to learn that the middle-aged-woman, half-her-age-hottie story line really was—in this case, alas—too good to be true. McMillan, now 54, filed for divorce in January, charging that Plummer, 31, hid from her the fact that he was gay and had married her for her money and the hope of gaining U.S. citizenship. "I have never felt such betrayal," she told PEOPLE. Plummer countered, saying that McMillan had turned on him in "homophobic" vengeance after he revealed his sexual preference in December 2004, claiming that he didn't know he was gay when he married her. With their divorce final Oct. 4, the two made a surprising appearance on *Oprah* Nov. 9. Asked if she still loved Plummer, McMillan said, "I love the man I married." When Oprah said, "Well, that ain't who he is now," McMillan did not disagree.

PARIS HILTON & NICOLE RICHIE AND PARIS HILTON & PARIS LATSIS

We'll always have Paris, but who will Paris have? In 2005 she got engaged, broke up and also split from erstwhile pal and *Simple Life* costar Nicole Richie

You knew their friendship was kaput April 15, when Paris, strutting down a Vegas runway to promote sister Nicky's fashion line, was flanked not by childhood pal Nicole but by new best bud Kimberly Stewart. Actually, "I knew months ago they weren't getting along," says a source close to both Hilton, 24, and Richie, 24. "They really hate each other." Why? Hilton's friends say Richie is jealous of the heavier media coverage—and higher pay (an estimated $5 million last season)—her *Simple Life* partner in mischief has reaped; Richie's camp claims Nicole has simply outgrown her wild ways and wants to settle down with fiancé Adam Goldstein.

For a while it looked as if Paris might beat her rival to the altar. In May she and Greek shipping scion Paris Latsis, 23, whom she began dating last December, announced their engagement and embarked on a two-month world tour. With fall came a chill, however. In September Hilton dropped her fiancé—albeit gently: "I will always love him," she said. "He treated me like a princess the entire time." Soon afterward she took up with another Greek shipping heir, Stavros Niarchos III. As for Paris and Nicole, there could be a solution to awkward moments on the *Simple Life* set: Season 4 of the series, to run on E! Entertainment, will film the reality stars' segments separately.

CHAD MICHAEL MURRAY & SOPHIA BUSH

Their marriage was canceled after five months, but they still play lovers on TV

If life went according to the script of *One Tree Hill*, Bush, 23, and Murray, 24, who play tempestuous, off-and-on lovers Brooke Davis and Lucas Scott on the WB teen drama, might still be an item. The couple, who fell in love on the set in 2003, exchanged handwritten vows at a seaside ceremony in Santa Monica April 16. "Chad was crying like a baby," says a guest. "Sophia cried too." Yet only five months later, they announced they were splitting. "This is a difficult and unfortunate situation," said Bush. A friend of hers was a bit more forthcoming: "Sophia went into the marriage believing in the sanctity of marriage, and Chad simply did not share that vision." The two, however, continued to share camera angles. An October storyline on *Hill* called for the recently estranged Brooke and Lucas to cozy up to each other. A tough act to pull off? So far, says an insider, Murray and Bush are "being professional. They know that whatever's happened to them in real life has to stay home."

SPIN CITY
Rumors that the couple (pictured pre-separation in 2003) would reconcile began swirling after Sheen's frequent public appearances with Richards and their two daughters.

MAKE UP?

E ven the couple's closest friends and family were surprised when a six-months-pregnant Richards, 34, filed for divorce from Sheen, 39, her husband of nearly three years and the father of their 11-month-old daughter Sam. Citing irreconcilable differences, Richards remained mum about the specifics behind the move, but sources close to her said she was concerned that Sheen had reverted to some of his bad-boy ways—a claim he vehemently denied at the time. "He did not cheat. He did not have a relapse. There is no scandal," said his rep Stan Rosenfield.

Despite Richards's continued statements that they were proceeding with the divorce, the *Two and a Half Men* star was in the delivery room when daughter Lola was born on June 1. The couple began to be seen out and about during the summer, and at a 65th-birthday party for his father, Martin, Richards gave Charlie a smooch. By October the divorce still hadn't been finalized, and Richards, too, stopped short of calling the union a write-off. "If our marriage could work out, it would be the ultimate blessing," she said. "If it can't, then Charlie and I will focus on being the best parents we can. So we'll see." Sheen was even more encouraging during a Nov. 3 appearance on CBS's *Late Late Show with Craig Ferguson,* flashing his wedding ring and announcing that "things are really good."

Charlie Sheen and Denise Richards split suddenly in March—then say they may reconcile

MOVING ON? Sheen packed up (left) from the couple's $1.6 million Agoura Hills, Calif., house and into a nearby residence several weeks before Richards filed for divorce in March. While they continued to live separately, the pair (right, in September 2005), who had been together since meeting on the set of *Spin City* in 2001, continued to take frequent outings with their kids as the year went on.

TIME'S UP

For Jessica Simpson and Nick Lachey, a TV show became a real-life soap opera with a sad ending

Jessica (with Nick at the MTV Music Awards in August) turned up a month later at a Manhattan magazine launch party without her husband—or her ring. "I left it on my bed stand," she said. "I'm forgetful."

They're head over heels for each other! They're estranged! They're together! They're faking it! They're more in love than ever!

Yes, it was a busy year for singers—and former reality-TV newlyweds—Nick Lachey, 32, and Jessica Simpson, 25. Rumors of discord flickered in January, with tales of Jessica partying, sans Nick, in Baton Rouge, where she was filming *The Dukes of Hazzard*. A month later, at a Super Bowl pregame party, a 6-ft. blonde female guest reportedly declined Nick's invitation, via a bodyguard, to a hotel-room rendezvous. (His rep said Lachey had done no such thing.) The night after the Super Bowl, the couple reunited at a Manhattan hot spot, dancing till the wee hours.

Still, signs of distress continued to pop up: Jessica arrived alone at the Emmys, and (on at least four occasions) she and Nick appeared in public without their wedding rings. In response to the negative buzz, Jessica's rep issued a statement: "Nick and Jessica have not separated. Rumors to the contrary are simply not true." As if to underscore that point, the couple, rings flashing, flew to Italy in early October to "do the romantic, Florence wine-tasting thing," said Nick. He suggested the visit was an advance celebration of their third anniversary, Oct. 26, which they would spend apart. (She went to Africa in support of a children's charity; he was at an undisclosed location, working on his album.)

Then, on Thanksgiving eve, the saga took another twist: "After three years of marriage, and careful thought and consideration, we have decided to part ways," the couple said in a joint statement. And thus the soap opera ended on a fittingly dramatic note.

GRIN AND BEAR IT
"Do they fight? Hell yes, they fight," said Jessica's dad, Joe Simpson, of the couple. "[But] if fighting is a sign of divorce, then we're all going to get divorced."

BIG AT THE
BOX
OFFICE

In a year when Hollywood was hurtin', these films packed surprising box-office power

BATMAN BEGINS

HOLY FRANCHISE FIXER!

Kryptonite? The Joker? The Green Goblin? As has been proven time and again, the only thing that can kill a superhero is bad box office. After *Batman & Robin* disappointed in 1997, the film franchise flatlined. Then came *Batman Begins*, starring Christian Bale as a tortured, even reluctant Caped Crusader. Among the darkest in the series, it nonetheless was hailed by critics and earned particular praise for its star. "Sleek as a panther," raved *The New York Times*, "Mr. Bale makes a superbly menacing avenger." And a superlative popcorn magnet: *Begins* begat $205 million at the box office.

A CHOCOLATE SURPRISE

The odds—and oddities—seemed stacked against the latest film remake of Roald Dahl's dark classic children's fable *Charlie and the Chocolate Factory*. But despite Johnny Depp's pageboy haircut and unintended resemblance to another man-child pied piper who welcomed kids to his private Neverland, *Charlie* charmed audiences with old-school humor and wondrous effects. And after scoring the biggest opening in Depp's career, *Charlie* banked $206 million in box office receipts.

THEY'RE MONEY

Whether bedding bridesmaids or trespassing in the holy sanctuaries of Jews, Irish, Italians and Hindus alike, there was something to offend almost everyone in *Wedding Crashers*. Aimed at adults who appreciate juvenile humor, the R-rated comedy starred Owen Wilson and Vince Vaughn as uninvited guests who just want to be loved—by as many members of the bridal party as possible. *Star Wars: Episode III—Revenge of the Sith* was the No. 1 film of the year, but *Crashers*—without spacemen or special effects—finished near the top.

CHARLIE AND THE CHOCOLATE FACTORY

WEDDING CRASHERS

DANCING WITH THE STARS

THE HIT PARADE

What people were talking about the next morning at the watercooler

LAGUNA BEACH

GREY'S ANATOMY

DANCING WITH THE STARS

It was a novel, nutty idea—a ballroom-dancing competition that teamed cha-cha pros and B-list celebs—and it worked. Spectacularly. An average of 17 million viewers tuned in to watch *General Hospital*'s Kelly Monaco, boxer Evander Holyfield and *Seinfeld*'s John O'Hurley, among others, go toe-to-toe and dip-for-dip for six summer weeks. When Monaco out-hoofed O'Hurley to take the title, skeptics accused ABC of rigging the vote in favor of the network's own soap star. Thus, the stage was set for the best dancing duel since *West Side Story*: In a September rematch, O'Hurley, master of the paso doble, vanquished Monaco.

LAGUNA BEACH

Was it real? Was it stage-managed? Did it matter? Set in Orange County, Calif., MTV's *Laguna* became a cult hit by weaving melodramatic yarns out of quintessential high school Sturm und Drang: boyfriends, parties, manicures. (For the record, *Laguna* golden girl Lauren "L.C." Conrad said, "I've never been handed a script.") By year's end, the little-cable-show-that-could was generating as much buzz as its network doppelganger, Fox's *The O.C.*

GREY'S ANATOMY

Who would dare to follow up *Desperate Housewives*? A riveting group of surgical residents. As soon as ABC's medical drama landed in the post-Wisteria Lane time slot, viewers' pulses started racing over the show's sly mix of life-and-death decision making and internecine romances. Plus, having Patrick Dempsey as the resident lover boy didn't hurt.

FINAL BOW

Beyoncé Knowles
(left) Michelle
Williams and Kelly
Rowland decided a
smooth exit was
their destiny.

After millions of CDs and many a makeover, a pop group leaves on a high note

DESTINY'S CHILD

Most groups, noted Destiny's Child supernova Beyoncé Knowles, "usually break up because they can't stand to be with each other. That's not the case" with her group, she added—needlessly. In Vancouver, where cofounding member Knowles, 24, Kelly Rowland, 24, and Michelle Williams, 25 (who joined in 2000), gave their farewell concert Sept. 10, the three friends shared a single dressing room, as they have since they began. Why? "Out of friendship, out of love," said Beyoncé, who was in tears by the end of the show, as were her partners. The trio have sold more than 40 million albums, with hits like their 1999 breakout "Bills, Bills, Bills." "Seeing the fans all lined up in the front row, it was very emotional," said Rowland. While they will no longer be sharing sugar-free Jell-O backstage, the three plan to get together to perform occasionally and stay close as friends. "Breakup sounds so final," said Beyoncé. "It's more a growing up."

NYPD BLUE

The boundary-pushing cop show handed in its badge

After 12 years, 20 Emmys and more naked posteriors than a *Police Gone Wild* video, *NYPD Blue* hung up its handcuffs. From the start, *Blue* was a different kind of cop show, exploring racism, alcoholism and other hot-button issues . But it was the nude scenes that often won the most attention, especially when star Dennis Franz (a four-time Emmy winner as Det. Andy Sipowicz) disrobed in Season 2. "That was done in response to people passing by on the streets and yelling, 'Yo, Sipowicz, when we gonna see your a—?' " recalled Franz, 60. As the final scene wrapped on Feb. 11, "it was a big weepfest around the place," said Franz "We realized what we were going to miss most was each other."

EVERYBODY LOVES RAYMOND

TV's hilariously dysfunctional family went out on top and got a goodbye gift from Emmy

For nine years they were one of TV's most-dependable laugh generators, but when it came time for *Everybody Loves Raymond* to say goodbye, there were nothing but tears to go around. "Before the [final] taping, I was like, 'I'm not going to cry,'" said Patricia Heaton, who played the take-no-sass wife of the show's titular star, Ray Romano. "Soon as we were done, I just sobbed my head off." Romano also lost it at the curtain call—the last time he and all of his costars (including Peter Boyle, Doris Roberts and Brad Garrett) would share the same soundstage. So why such emotion from the Barone clan? Roberts, who played Romano's nosy mom, summed it up best: "It was nine glorious years of working with people who liked each other." Even more love came their way after the show wrapped: Roberts won her fourth Best Supporting Actress Emmy, and the show nabbed Best Comedy for its swan-song season.

The 23-year-old racing rookie revved up the Indy 500 by giving the guys a real run for the title

DANICA PATRICK

With a quick "Lady and gentlemen, start your engines," the 89th running of the Indianapolis 500 began its full-throttled lurch into the history books. Twenty-three-year-old Danica Patrick made a serious run for the $1.5 million prize money, leading the field—the first woman in Indy history to do so—before a dwindling fuel supply forced her to lighten up on the pedal with six laps to go. "I thought for a second we were going to win this thing," said Patrick, who finished fourth. Still, the 5'2" phenom turbocharged the event (TV ratings jumped 40 percent from 2004) and set herself up for an endorsement jackpot. Maybe she'll rep the pink nail polish she's been known to wear? "That's the yin and yang of Danica," said 1986 Indy champ Bobby Rahal, who with *Late Show* host David Letterman co-owns the team that sponsors Patrick. "The exterior is nice and pretty—and underneath she is as tough as steel." She's also got a sixth sense for the sport. "When we're going 200-plus mph, I can see things happening and have time to react," Patrick told PEOPLE. "I think that is a special gift."

This was the year that the TV-catchphrase hall of fame—home to stale slogans of yesteryear like "Sit on it!" and "Kiss my grits!"—was forced to make room for a bold new attraction: "Hug it out, bitch!" When uttered by HBO's *Entourage* star Jeremy Piven—who plays high-strung, expensive-suited, expletive-never-deleted Hollywood agent Ari Gold—the phrase (used in moments of extreme male bonding) packed enough comedic resonance to earn a place in TV history. Although Piven is no stranger to TV (he was a costar on Ellen DeGeneres's sitcom back in 1995, headlined the ill-fated ABC comedy *Cupid* in 1998 and has had a bevy of guest-starring roles), his tour-de-force take on the Tinseltown shark was so finely nuanced it was as if he had finally found a bespoke role in an often off-the-rack medium.

JEREMY PIVEN

The *Entourage* star
added bite to the role of
a Hollywood shark

TERRENCE HOWARD

A starring role in *Hustle & Flow* showcased his rhyme and his reason

Back in 2001, *The New York Times* called him "the best actor you've never heard of." This year—fresh from a scene-stealing turn in *Crash*—Terrence Howard scored big in the follow-your-dream hip-hop drama *Hustle & Flow*. "He has

so much depth," said producer John Singleton. "You know there's something going on in his head." Elsewhere as well: "I lend my flesh to a role," Howard said. "I'm not going to just lend the bones."

Howard, who grew up in

Cleveland, is twice married—to the same woman. "I was a boy in a man's frame" when he and Lori first wed and later divorced, he said. Since remarrying in February, however, the two reportedly had split once again by year's end.

CLASS OF '05

Most likely to not order an extra-large dessert in the school cafeteria LINDSAY LOHAN & NICOLE RICHIE

Is It Hollywood

Most passionate PDA
MARY-KATE & STAVROS

Dating the deejay
NICOLE AND
DJ AM

Prom Queen and King
PARIS & PARIS

OMG! Drama! Drama! Drama! DRAMA!!!!!

You know how Nicole and Paris have been BFFs since, like, the days before reality TV was invented and now they suddenly started hating on each other? Paris is all like, "Nicole knows what she did" and Nicole is all like, "We really haven't been friends in probably about two years!" And Nicole used to be kind of normal-size but now she's so not, and she actually got engaged to her deejay boyfriend (who used to weigh, like, 300 lbs. but now, again, sooo not). Paris got engaged too—to a guy who's also named Paris (random!). He was one of the hot new foreign-exchange kids—from, like, Greece or someplace bizarro—but then his parents were kind of being jerks so she bailed and then she started macking on this other foreign-exchange kid Stavros (also from Greece—doubly random!!!!!), who used to be all hot and heavy with Mary-Kate (they did fun stuff like make out on a trampoline). But now he's doing fun stuff (like riding dune buggies on the beach) with Paris.

or High School?

You make the call!

MISCHA WITH BRANDON DAVIS (BEFORE),
MISCHA AND CISCO ADLER (AFTER)

Here's the Mischa scoop: After she
and Brandon broke up, she totally
hooked up with Kimberly's rocker-dude
ex Cisco. Then Kimberly started
acting out and got close to this older
guy who makes money by videotaping
girls taking their tops off. A couple
months later and she's engaged to
that surfer dude Talan.

And get this: You know that goofy guy Ashton, who punks everyone? He went and got married to ...Ms. Moore!!!! Who is only, like, the Hottest Homeroom Teacher in Recorded History! OMG OMG OMG!!!!!!!! At first everyone thought it was weird. But you know? They're really a cute couple. And his grades have gone up.

They went and did it!
MR. AND MRS. ASHTON KUTCHER

Before the breakup
WILMER AND LINDSAY

And Lindsay, after breaking up with her boyfriend, dyed her hair and got really skinny and went to parties and crashed her car, like, a thousand bazillion times — but now she's, like, you know, fine.

BEST & WORST

Little black dresses took a time-out this year, as rich colors, formfitting shapes, and divine details turned red-carpet couture into something bold and beautiful. But when trends were taken *too* far (brassy hues, overexposed flesh and busy extras), the effect went from bedazzling to bewildering

CATE BLANCHETT
The *Aviator* star walked
away with Best Supporting
Actress honors wearing
Valentino Couture. "I decided
to have one special dress
conceived for this one special
actress," said the designer

CHARLIZE THERON
in Dior Haute Couture

SALMA HAYEK
in Prada

HALLE BERRY
in Atelier Versace

THE ACADEMY AWARDS

KIRSTEN DUNST
in Chanel

OPRAH WINFREY
in Vera Wang

GWYNETH PALTROW
in Stella McCartney

HILARY SWANK
in Calvin Klein

TERI HATCHER
in Donna Karan

CHARLIZE THERON
in Dior by John Galliano

THE
GOLDEN
GLOBE
AWARDS

EVA LONGORIA
in Oscar de la Renta

SCARLETT JOHANSSON
in Roland Mouret

NICOLE KIDMAN
in Gucci

THE
EMMY
AWARDS

HALLE BERRY
in Ungaro

JENNIFER GARNER
in Badgley Mischka

MARISKA HARGITAY
in Carolina Herrera

TERI HATCHER
in J. Mendel

MARCIA CROSS
in Elie Saab Couture

MISCHA BARTON
in Oscar de la Renta

JESSICA ALBA
in Giorgio Armani Privé

CATHERINE ZETA-JONES
in Dolce & Gabbana

SIENNA MILLER
in Dior by John Galliano

PREMIERE LOOKS

ANGELINA JOLIE
in Versace

KEIRA KNIGHTLEY
in Matthew Williamson

KATE HUDS
in Roberto Ca

PUT ON YOUR PARTY DRESS

BEYONCE
in Dolce & Gabbana

SARAH JESSICA PARKER
in Oscar de la Renta

CLAIRE DANES
in Calvin Klein

AMERIE
in Monique Lhuillier

NAOMI WATTS
in Calvin Klein

NICOLE RICHIE
in Moschino Couture

MELANIE GRIFFITH
A surfeit of sequins?

MARIAH CAREY
The Little Mermaid's Junior Prom?

SHERYL CROW
Shark-bite style

ON THE OTHER HAND...

TYRA BANKS
Dream date for the Aflac duck?

MELISSA GEORGE
Too much? Check.

NICOLLETTE SHERIDAN
Sherbet not a sure bet?

THAT'S SO 2005

Like '70s platform shoes and '80s shoulder pads: Five accessories you'll someday use to date old photos

BIG BEADS
The tribal trend seen on fashion runways inspired several celebs including Jessica Simpson, proudly garlanded with Hawaiian kukui nuts in L.A. And her eyewear of choice? Big sunglasses.

COWBOY BOOTS

They're as American as deep-fried Snickers, but fashionistas credit their revival to chic Brit actress Sienna Miller. Lindsay Lohan and Nicole Richie wore theirs with . . . big sunglasses.

TUNIC

The sparklier the better. Here this season's must-have top, a red-carpet regular, runs errands with Halle Berry . . . and big sunglasses.

PEASANT SKIRT

Long, flowy skirts competed with jeans as the go-anywhere item. Even Paris Hilton stepped out with peasants and . . . big sunglasses.

OVERSIZE SUNGLASSES

Hey you, eight-eyes! Either the Olsen twins—who some say started the trend—are kinda small or those are really, really . . . big sunglasses.

GIVING BACK

In a year of disasters, some celebs stepped up and tried to lend a hand

ANGELINA JOLIE Pakistan

"I'd like to die feeling that I've been useful," said Jolie. The UNHCR (United Nations High Commissioner for Refugees) goodwill ambassador made humanitarian trips to Ethiopia, Sierra Leone and Pakistan, where she visited with an Afghan boy (right) and climbed a truck to talk with female refugees (below).

PETRA NEMCOVA
Thailand
After the death of her boy-friend, photographer Simon Atlee, and breaking her pelvis in the South Asia tsunami, the Czech model returned to Thailand in April to visit schoolchildren and thank the medical staff at the hospital where she was treated.

CLAY AIKEN
Indonesia
As a **UNICEF** ambassador, the *American Idol* star traveled to Indonesia and Malaysia to visit *tsunami* victims, and to Uganda to help displaced children who had fled the country's rebel militia. "I cried for two hours over how catastrophic this was," he said of that visit.

RICKY MARTIN
Thailand
"It was impossible for me to stay home with my arms crossed," said Martin, who handed out chocolates and beef jerky in January to children affected by the tsunami. "You try to see [the human spirit.]"

BRAD [PITT] South Africa

To raise awareness about AIDS and economic reform, Pitt made a goodwill trip to Africa on behalf of Bono's campaign DATA. Among the highlights: dancing and singing with kids in Ethiopia. "This is just the beginning for me," said Pitt.

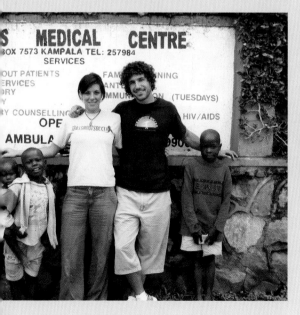

ETHAN ZOHN & JENNA MORASCA Uganda

"Ethan laughed because I was giving away Dolce & Gabbana shirts," said Morasca of the *Survivor* sweethearts' 10-day trip. Their mission was more serious: to educate children about AIDS through Zohn's organization Grassroot Soccer. "[Zohn's] got a big, big heart," said Morasca. "He's saving lives, and that's a feat in itself."

JOHNNY CARSON

For 30 years the wry magician from Nebraska told jokes, touched lives and tucked America in

Of all the stars spawned by the tube, declared an uncharacteristically un-glib David Letterman at the 2005 Emmy Awards in September, none "meant as much to the daily lives of the people of this country for as long as Johnny Carson." Or, as the *Tonight Show* host's sidekick and friend Ed McMahon spelled it out for PEOPLE: "You got up, you had breakfast, you went to your job and came home, you had a couple of drinks and dinner and you watched Carson and you went to bed. That was the routine. If you were lucky, you had wild sex."

Carson, though, was a tonic, not an aphrodisiac. From Oct. 1, 1962, when, at 36, the Norfolk, Neb.-born magician turned game-show host took over *Tonight,* until his final broadcast, on May 22, 1992, the talk king reigned with charm, grace and, of course, humor. "Johnny's monologue was like *The New York Times,*"

"Sis boom bah . . . What is the sound of a sheep exploding?" went a bit when Carson (in 1963) played Carnac the Magnificent (below).

Letterman said. "It was the nightly television comedy of record. And if a joke bombed, with a sly look of withering disdain Johnny made that the funniest moment of the night."

Carson turned his host's desk—a flimsy prop table—into the holy grail for several generations of comedians, from Woody Allen and George Carlin to Billy Crystal and Jerry Seinfeld. And a greenroom full of future talk-show hosts, including Letterman, Jay Leno, Conan O'Brien and Ellen DeGeneres, studied him like a treasure map. "Anyone who does this for a living," said O'Brien, "is trying in vain to be Johnny Carson."

Married four times and the father of three sons with first wife Jody (their middle child, Rick, was killed in a car accident the year before Carson left the show), Carson never returned to TV after retiring at 66. He spent most of the ensuing years in self-imposed exile in his $12 million Malibu home, or sailing his beloved yacht, *Serengeti,* with his fourth wife, Alexis, a former secretary whom he wed in 1987. Throughout, he stayed close to comedian pals and poker buddies like Steve Martin and Carl Reiner and continued to supply jokes to Letterman. He would even entertain friends with informal monologues based on the latest headlines. "He would do a full routine," said one friend. "He was hysterical. It was as if he had to perform." A lifelong smoker, Carson died of complications of emphysema Jan. 23. The man whose intro ("Heeere's Johnny!") had long since entered the pop lexicon had once offered his preferred epitaph: "I'll be right back."

On his final show, Bette Midler sang her tribute: "I watched your hair turn from dark to white/ And when I can't sleep, I count your wives at night . . ."

'JOHNNY BLOSSOMED [ONSTAGE] AND BECAME A FOOT TALLER, POWERFUL—LIKE HE OWNED THE WORLD'
—*TONIGHT SHOW* BOOKER BOB SHAYNE

Honoring a lifetime spent promoting peace, the world paid its respects to the man hailed as the People's Pope

POPE
JOHN PAUL II

By the time he died at 9:37 on the night of April 2, John Paul II had touched so many lives that it was hard to remember a world without him—the boy from a Polish town who rose to lead the billion-member Roman Catholic Church during an era of immense change. Almost immediately after his death (according to the Vatican, the pontiff's last words were, "Let me go to the house of the Father"), the outpouring began, with heads of state and ordinary followers eulogizing the man who had been at the head of the Catholic Church since October 1978. "Pope John Paul II was unquestionably the most influential voice for morality and peace in the world during the last 100 years," said the Reverend Billy Graham. "He was respected by men and women from every conceivable background across the world."

At his last public appearance from his window over St. Peter's Square, he was so sick that he couldn't speak. It didn't matter; Pope John Paul II had long since gotten his message out. That much was obvious on April 8, during his funeral in St. Peter's Square, from the sea of placards and chants demanding "Santo Subito" ("Sainthood Now") to the legions of world leaders, including both Presidents Bush, former President Clinton and hundreds of international dignitaries. It was clear, too, in the hearts of countless mourners like Mary Dortie, a London civil servant who stayed up all night to be in the square because "it was my chance to say goodbye, not to one of the greatest but to the greatest Pope." In his homily Cardinal Joseph Ratzinger, one of the Pope's closest advisers—and the man who, as Benedict XVI, became, at 78, his successor on April 24—said that John Paul now stands at God's window, "where he sees us and blesses us."

ANNE
BANCROFT

Here's to you, Mrs. Robinson:
The versatile actress seduced
a generation of moviegoers as
The Graduate's purring vixen

She'd won an Oscar as Helen Keller's savior in *The Miracle Worker* and accolades for a half-century career on Broadway and in Hollywood. But it was for her role as the husky-voiced suburban matron who seduces half-her-age Dustin Hoffman in 1967's *The Graduate* that she was best known. "I'm just a little dismayed," she once said, "that people aren't past [Mrs. Robinson] yet." Bronx-born as Anna Maria Louisa Italiano, the actress—married to husband Mel Brooks for 40 years—died of uterine cancer at 73 in June. "She was so warm and generous and sweet," said her *Keeping the Faith* costar Jenna Elfman, "and a complete toughie all at the same time."

1931-2005

With a velvety voice and elegant style, the R&B legend sang the songs that put fans in the mood

LUTHER
VANDROSS

So many people had babies because of Luther," Patti LaBelle said of her good friend, whose seductive vocals practically demanded to be played in the bedroom. His songs "made you want to just make love and be happy." Gracious, witty and impeccably style-conscious—he never took to the stage in anything but a tuxedo—Luther Vandross started off as a backup singer for the likes of David Bowie, Bette Midler and Barbra Streisand before breaking out as a solo superstar with the 1981 single "Never Too Much." He went on to sell 30 million albums and nab eight Grammy Awards. But even as his professional life thrived, Vandross battled health problems, including diabetes, hypertension and obesity; his weight fluctuated from 180 to 320 lbs. In 2003 he suffered a debilitating stroke, which left him in a coma for six weeks. Two years later, while recuperating, he died during a physical therapy session. The Reverend Jesse Jackson, a friend, described him as "a boy so mellow, so powerful; a boy of rare, rare vintage." Said LaBelle: "He had the one and only voice like that in the world."

1951-2005

PETER JENNINGS

Covering war or battling cancer, ABC's anchor showed courage under fire

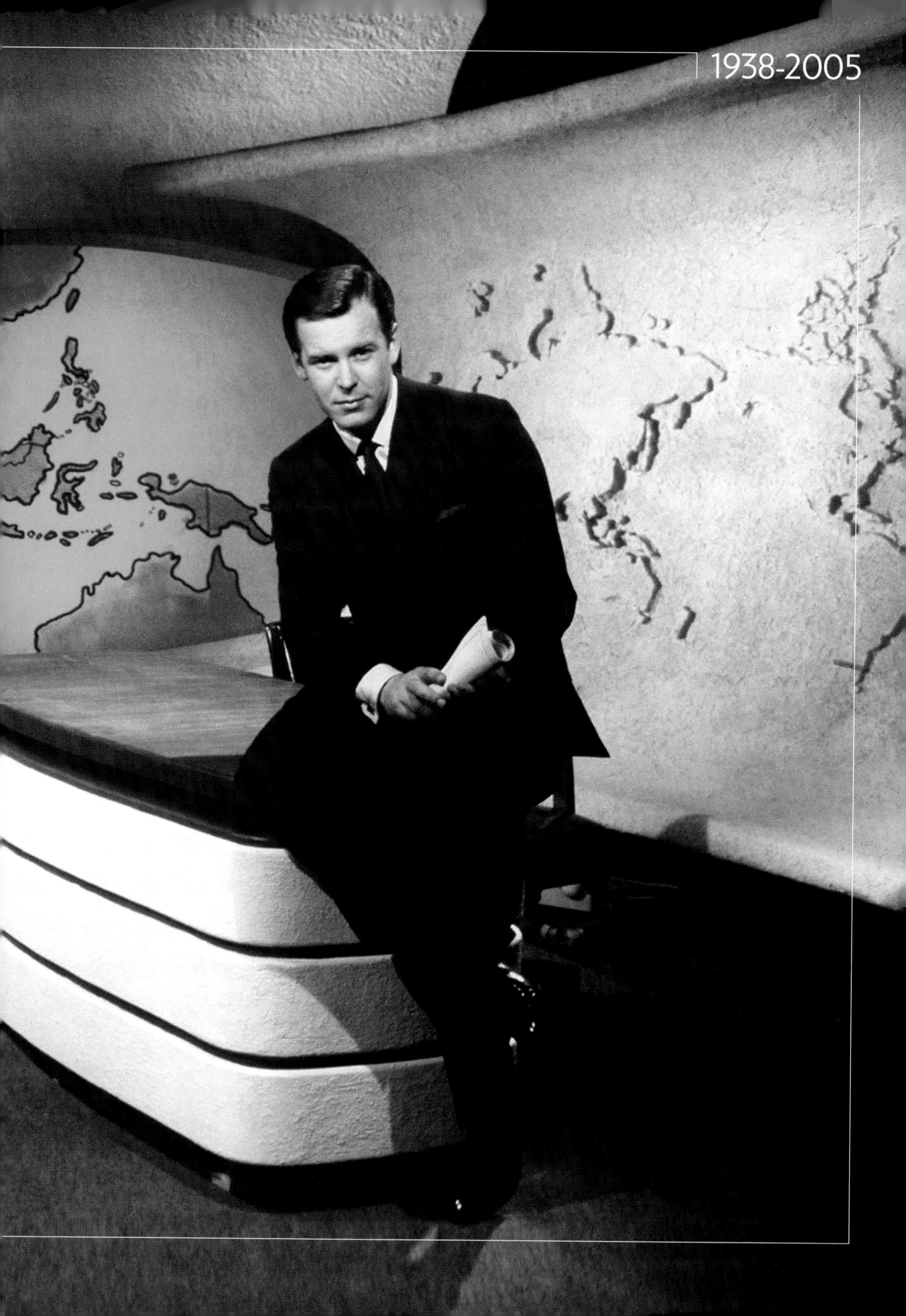

One of the strangest facts about Peter Jennings? He was a high-school dropout. The son of a Canadian Broadcasting Corporation executive, Jennings landed his first on-air gig at the age of 9—as the host of a children's radio show—and ultimately ditched the diploma route to stay on the broadcasting fast track. In 1962 he became an anchor on Canada's first commercial network news program. Two years later, at age 26, ABC News recruited him to anchor its then-15-minute newscast. Up against CBS's Walter Cronkite and NBC's Huntley and Brinkley, Jennings proved a ratings disaster. But after more than 15 years as a roving foreign correspondent for ABC (he opened the first U.S. TV-news bureau in the Middle East), he was back at the helm in 1983 and ultimately propelled *World News Tonight* to No. 1 over Tom Brokaw and Dan Rather.

Throughout his career, Jennings, who died Aug. 7, became known for his dogged pursuit of a story. He traveled to the far reaches of the globe, stayed on the air for 24-plus hours (as he did during ABC's Millennium 2000 coverage and during 9/11) and hounded prickly statesmen like Yasser Arafat to sit down for interviews. "People compared him to James

ANCHOR AWAY

The well-traveled newsman loved getting out from behind the desk to land a high-profile scoop.

With the Ayatollah Khomeini in 1979.

Strolling with Anwar Sadat in 1974.

Hosting a town-hall with President Clinton (and Chelsea and Socks) in 1993.

Bond," said one ABC News correspondent. "This was a guy who'd been in war zones and natural disasters, and he just came through looking cool and collected."

Typically, when Peter Jennings himself became news, he delivered it first-hand. "I have learned in the last couple of days that I have lung cancer," he announced in a scratchy voice on what would be his final *World News Tonight* telecast on April 5. Even after his diagnosis, the avid newsman joined in *WNT* story meetings via teleconference. Said colleague Ted Koppel: "He continued to be the living embodiment of ABC News until the day he died."

1924-2005

SHIRLEY CHISHOLM

The first black woman elected to Congress knocked down barriers and stuck up for the little guy

When Shirley Chisholm won election in 1968, she was sometimes greeted in Washington with cold shoulders rather than open arms. Nonetheless, using the motto "Unbought and Unbossed," she became an advocate for the disenfranchised during the 14 years she represented her New York City district. In 1972 Chisholm—who died after suffering a series of strokes—became the first black woman to make a major-party bid for the Presidency, although she admitted it was a largely symbolic effort. "When I die," she said, "I want to be remembered as a woman who lived in the 20th century and who dared to be a catalyst for change."

Chisholm (in 1975) once advised a friend, "If they don't give you a seat at the table, bring in a folding chair."

1937-2005

"I hate to advocate drugs, alcohol, violence or insanity to anyone, but they've always worked for me," quoth Thompson (at home in 1991).

HUNTER S. THOMPSON

The king of gonzo chronicled the sinister and the absurd in American politics and life with savage grace and scathing humor

People like him," reckoned a biographer, "because he said all the stuff everybody wishes they could say." But it was the outrageous way Hunter S. Thompson said it that gave birth to his patented "gonzo" journalism in provocative literary grenades like *The Kentucky Derby Is Decadent and Depraved* and *Fear and Loathing in Las Vegas: A Savage Journey to the Heart of the American Dream.*

When William McKeen published his 1991 biography, Thompson, recalled the author, "sent a fax saying, 'I warned you not to write that vicious trash about me. How fast can you get fitted for an eye patch in case one of your eyes gets gouged out?' That was his way of saying, 'You did a nice job.'"

Not surprisingly, he made a gonzo exit. Nearly crippled and in physical pain after decades of flamboyant drug and alcohol abuse, Thompson,

67, paid gruesome homage to his hero Ernest Hemingway by shooting himself in the head in his Woody Creek, Colo., home.

In accordance with his wishes—and with second wife Anita and son Juan, as well as celeb pals like Bill Murray, Sen. John Kerry, George McGovern and Johnny Depp (who paid for the $2 million Aug. 20 ceremony), looking on—Thompson's ashes were fired out of a cannon into the Colorado sky.

SANDRA DEE

Goodbye Gidget: For the movies' teen
dream girl, growing up was hard to do

Look at me, I'm Sandra Dee, lousy with virginity,"
Stockard Channing sang in the 1978 film *Grease*.
With her bouncy beauty and flirty, G-rated sexi-
ness, Dee starred in frothy comedies like *Gidget* and
Tammy Tell Me True and became a teen icon of the late
1950s and early '60s. As much as she enjoyed Channing's spoof a decade later—"She thought it was fun,"
said a friend—Dee was by then mired in a downward spi-
ral of alcohol abuse that began as her star faded in the
mid-'60s. Born Alexandria Zuck in Bayonne, N.J., Dee
was 16 when she married crooner Bobby Darin, then 24.
Her love, if not their marriage, which lasted seven years
and produced a son, endured. A friend said of Dee, who
died Feb. 20, at 60, of kidney disease, Darin remained
"the love of her life until the day she died."

"She put up a good
fight," a friend said
of Dee (in 1959)
and her battle with
alcoholism.

JOHNNIE COCHRAN

1937-2005

The shrewd, eloquent lawyer behind O.J. Simpson's "not guilty"

To be sure, his fame rested on his skillful (some would say cynical) raising of racial issues in getting O.J. Simpson acquitted of murder. But "the clients I've cared about the most are the No-J's," Cochran once said, exhibiting his trademark gift for aphorism, "the ones who nobody knows." Cochran, who died of a brain tumor on March 29, first made his name by taking on the LAPD in a series of high-profile police-brutality cases. As much as the victories, he loved the process—and being at center stage. "The day you stop looking forward to the mystery and challenge of every tomorrow," he told *Court TV* anchor Jami Floyd, "is when you stop living."

At the O.J. Simpson trial, Cochran famously said of a glove in evidence, "If it doesn't fit, you must acquit."

1908-2005

SIMON WIESENTHAL

A Holocaust survivor made human rights his mission

From 1945, when he was liberated from the Mauthausen concentration camp at 36, until his death Sept. 20 in Vienna, Wiesenthal never rested in his pursuit of the murderers of 6 million Jews (among them his mother and 88 relatives) and millions of others during World War II. In his later years, Wiesenthal also worked to raise awareness of other war crimes, such as the Rwandan genocide. Such, he believed, was a survivor's burden. "A last witness, before he leaves this world, has an obligation to speak out," he told PEOPLE in 1988. "My work is a warning for the murderers of tomorrow."

1924-2005

OSSIE DAVIS

The actor and activist
blazed trails on two fronts

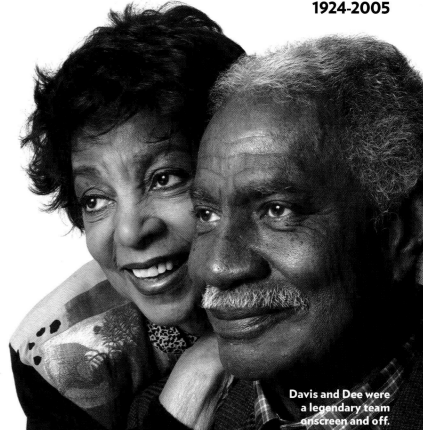

Davis and Dee were
a legendary team
onscreen and off.

Y ou could just look at him and see the
whole of where we come from and
where we are," said Oscar nominee Don
Cheadle (*Hotel Rwanda*) of Ossie Davis,
the avuncular actor with a commanding
baritone who inspired generations of
black actors with his prolific career. A
friend of both Martin Luther King Jr.'s
and Malcolm X's, Davis—who died of natural causes on Feb. 4—was an indefa-
tigable civil rights activist who unleashed
his eloquence at countless rallies, including the 1963 March on Washington,
which he helped organize. But it was his
partnership with his wife of 56 years, actress Ruby Dee, that his admirers remember most fondly. "They're like one word,
ossiedavisandrubydee," said friend
Denzel Washington at a Harlem tribute.
"They were always an example to me."

"Bellow fit the
whole world
on the page,"
novelist Dave
Eggers once
said of his
literary hero
(in 1962).

1915-2005

SAUL BELLOW

An émigré hailed as an
American original

T here's no telling what Nobel-
winning novelist Saul Bellow's
reaction would have been to Philip
Roth, who placed him in the pantheon
of great American writers, right along-
side Melville, Hawthorne and Twain.
But when Joyce Carol Oates deemed
him a genius, Bellow deadpanned, "I
tend to agree with her."

"I am an American, Chicago born,"
he wrote in *The Adventures of Augie
March*. A few facts aside—he was born
in Quebec but bred, from age 9, in
Chicago—his novels, including his 1976
Pulitzer winner, *Humboldt's Gift*, were,
in essence, all a form of autobiography.
In them, said Bellow, who died at 89 of
undisclosed causes April 5, he wrestled
with "what we human beings are . . .
what this life is for."

PHILIP JOHNSON
1906-2005

The dean of American architects delighted in shattering the mold

Philip Johnson loved nothing better than to confound expectations—except when it came to lunch. For decades the dapper man in the owlish glasses had a standing 12:30 reservation at the best table in New York City's power-loaded Four Seasons restaurant, a masterpiece of modernist architecture that he happened also to have designed, in 1959. Johnson's death on Jan. 25 leaves an empty seat at the Four Seasons and a void in the realm of American architecture. Over half a century, Johnson became the dean of his craft, with his work evolving from glass-box skyscrapers—and his own shockingly minimal 1949 Glass House in Connecticut, where he lived with his partner of 45 years, art dealer David Whitney—to postmodern towers with flamboyant flourishes. "There is only one absolute today," Johnson once noted, "and that is change."

1915-2005

ARTHUR MILLER

He dramatized American tragedies and loved one of Hollywood's most glamorous—and tragic—figures

He wrote in his autobiography that he wanted "to save America, and that meant grabbing people and shaking them by the back of the neck." Arthur Miller did that with *Death of a Salesman*—his searing, 1949 Pulitzer Prize-winning tragedy—and with *The Crucible*, his brave allegory of McCarthy-era hysteria, in 1953. He also fed the nation's fantasies by wedding sex goddess Marilyn Monroe in 1956. After their marriage ended in 1961, "he didn't want to talk about Marilyn," said actor Eli Wallach, a friend. But he did write about her—in his 1964 play *After the Fall*. And his final work, 2004's *Finishing the Picture*, was based on the filming of *The Misfits*, a movie he wrote for her. Miller—who died of congestive heart failure at 89, surrounded by family (including writer-director Rebecca, the youngest of his four children, and her husband, Daniel Day-Lewis) in his Roxbury, Conn., farmhouse—was, said director Nicholas Hytner, "the last of the great titans of the American stage."

JACKIE DONAHUE

Nelly's half sister (and stylist) helped fellow leukemia sufferers

Before going onstage in Beaumont, Texas, on March 24, rapper Nelly got the call he had long been dreading. His half sister Jackie Donahue, 31, had lost a four-year battle with leukemia, two years after the pair launched a foundation to raise awareness of bone-marrow donation. "They were always close," says his cousin Yomi Martin. "I don't think Nelly thought he'd be gone and not be able to say goodbye. This broke his heart." Donahue, who had the same father as Nelly and worked as his stylist, was diagnosed with acute myelogenous leukemia in March 2001 and was told she needed a bone-marrow transplant when she relapsed two years later. Although she never found a match, one of her relatives, aided by the foundation, did receive a life-saving transplant. Said Jackie's mom, Sarah Donahue: "Jackie was so pleased by that."

ROSE MARY WOODS

A loyal secretary best remembered for acrobatics

Richard Nixon called her "the most discreet woman in the world." Which was why, after 23 years of loyal service to the man she called the Boss, Rose Mary Woods's most public act—demonstrating in Watergate judge John J. Sirica's courtroom how she supposedly erased 18½ minutes from a crucial White House tape—was so excruciating. Her awkward contortions became known as "the Rose Mary Woods stretch." Implausible as the court—and American public—found Woods's explanation, it could not be disproved. More painful for Woods, perhaps, was the final act she performed for the Boss on the eve of his departure from the White House: She, not Nixon, told his family of his decision to resign the Presidency. Woods, who never married, died Jan. 20 of undisclosed causes in Alliance, Ohio.

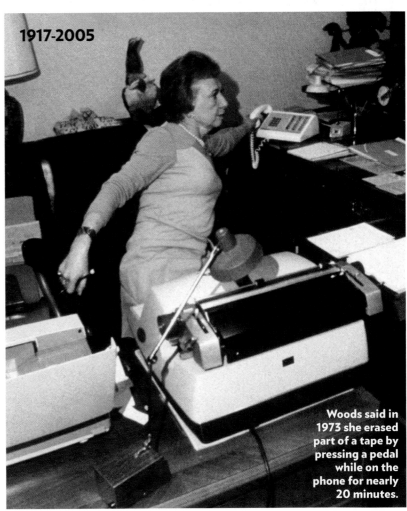

1917-2005

Woods said in 1973 she erased part of a tape by pressing a pedal while on the phone for nearly 20 minutes.

1906-2005

Oliver Douglas **EDDIE ALBERT**

He was best known for playing the countryside-loving straight man to Eva Gabor's ditzy, city-craving socialite on *Green Acres,* but "acting was really only a tenth of his life," says Edward Albert of his dad, Eddie Albert. He got his acting break in the 1938 movie *Brother Rat,* then joined the Navy during World War II, earning a Bronze Star for rescuing wounded Marines. In the 1970s, he became an outspoken environmentalist. The veteran of more than 200 films and TV shows (he earned an Oscar nomination for playing Gregory Peck's sidekick in 1953's *Roman Holiday*) suffered from Alzheimer's, but "up till the end, his intellect was intact," says his son. "He [even] took up singing. He said he was getting ready for his next life."

1933-2005

The Riddler
FRANK GORSHIN

He was the first impressionist to become a [Las Vegas] headliner," recalled fellow mimic Rich Little of Frank Gorshin, whose knack for aping the likes of Cary Grant and James Cagney earned him fame in the '60s. He made his biggest impression, however, as the Riddler on the campy '60s TV series *Batman*: His dramatic flair turned the archvillain into classic TV. Gorshin, who died of lung cancer, also proved there was more beneath the lime-green jumpsuit: He got an Emmy nomination for a guest role on *Star Trek* and won kudos for a one-man stage show about George Burns, which ended in April. "He said to me, 'I could play Burns till the day I died.'" said Little. "Which is what he did."

1920-2005   Scotty **JAMES DOOHAN**

He was a beautiful, irascible man," said Nichelle Nichols (Uhura) of *Star Trek* castmate James Doohan, who played the starship *Enterprise*'s always-frantic chief engineer, Montgomery "Scotty" Scott. A Vancouver native who served in WWII (he lost a finger to machine-gun fire), Doohan was unable to break free of his Scotty typecasting, so he embraced his fate, appearing in the *Trek* film franchise and making personal appearances. In July, he succumbed to pneumonia and complications from Alzheimer's disease. Doohan's Trekkie legacy lived on: His wife had Doohan's ashes shot into space in December. "He was such a down-to-earth guy," said *Trek*'s George Takei (Sulu), "but now he'll be in the galaxies."

Maxwell Smart **DON ADAMS**

Would you believe Don Adams was nothing like Maxwell Smart, the klutzy secret agent he played in the '60s TV spy spoof *Get Smart*? "He was not at all the bumbling idiot," said costar Barbara Feldon. "Don was extremely intelligent. He was interested in history; he used to write poetry." For fans of Adams's, the poetry was in his staccato, nasal delivery of lines like, "Sorry about that, Chief." A WWII Marine veteran who fought on Guadalcanal, Adams—who died of a lung infection—started out as a stand-up comic and later worked as a voice actor (*Inspector Gadget*). But his true genius was in playing dumb. "Don was really smart," said *Get Smart* co-creator Mel Brooks. "Not Maxwell Smart—he was Don Adams smart."

1923-2005

1935-2005 Gilligan **BOB DENVER**

As the lovably inept castaway on the 1960s TV hit *Gilligan's Island,* he would set his pants on fire, thwonk the Skipper with a boomerang and tangle himself up in a hammock. In real life Bob Denver "was the opposite of the goofy guy he played," said friend and castmate Russell Johnson (the Professor). But "he wasn't the opposite in terms of sweetness, generosity and kindness." Denver—who died from complications from cancer treatment—was also beloved for his portrayal of Maynard G. Krebs, the beatnik sidekick on TV's *The Many Loves of Dobie Gillis*. "As an actor he saw the world through the eyes of a child," said *Island* costar Dawn Wells (Mary Ann). "As a person he had intellect and wisdom in his soul."

PRINCE RAINIER

His love for a movie queen
made her a real-life princess

His kingdom was no larger than New York City's Central Park. But during his 55-year reign, Prince Rainier III of Monaco transformed the tiny Riviera principality from a sleepy casino town into a glittering resort and financial center. Monaco—famously described by Somerset Maugham as "a sunny place for shady people"—got a huge publicity upgrade in 1956, when more than 30 million viewers watched broadcasts and newsreels of the 32-year-old prince's lavish wedding to 26-year-old American movie star Grace Kelly. The actress, whom Rainier had met at the Cannes Film Festival the year before, was, said her bridesmaid, "a total vision" in a gown of rose-point lace and 100 yards of silk net. "It was a once-in-a-lifetime event."

And a highlight of Rainier's storybook life. The product of a prince-and-pauper union between a French nobleman and a laundress who happened to be the illegitimate daughter of Prince Louis II of Monaco, Rainier inherited the throne in 1949. His charmed reign was struck by tragedy in 1982, when Princess Grace, 52, was killed in a car crash while driving with 17-

year-old daughter Stephanie—one of the couple's three headline-grabbing progeny—on a steep mountain road near Monaco. "Part of Rainier died with her," said biographer Jeffrey Robinson. Once asked if he considered remarrying, Rainier—who died of multiple organ failure April 6 at 81—replied, "How could I? Everywhere I go, I see Grace."

1923-2005

SHELBY FOOTE

He helped turn history into must-see TV

"There's nothing better for a writer than to be reluctant to go to bed, anxious to wake up and start again," said novelist, historian and unlikely TV star Shelby Foote. "That's living."

Foote did a whole lot of it. For 20 years he scratched 500 words a day with an old-fashioned dip pen—it "reduces the hell out of the need for rewriting," he said—to produce his masterpiece, a three-volume history, *The Civil War: A Narrative*. As engaging as any novel, the book captured the epic sweep of the war he called "the central event of our history" and offered sabre-sharp sketches of characters as familiar as Lincoln and Lee and as obscure as the barefoot Confederate soldiers and frightened Yankee conscripts who peopled his pages.

It was not his writing, however, but his courtly manner and honey-and-magnolia-steeped eloquence that made Foote, a Greenville, Miss., native, a star. As principal commentator of Ken Burns's 11-hour 1990 PBS series *The Civil War*, Foote enthralled millions of viewers with his masterly storytelling. Burns called him "the presiding spirit of the documentary." Fans, some with marriage proposals, called him at home (his number was listed in the phone book in Memphis, where he lived with his third wife, Gwyn). "When I was a hardworking, pistol-hot writer, I was unknown," said Foote, who died of heart failure in June. "Now that I'm a tired old man, they start hollerin' how good I am." Not that all the "hoorah"—his term for fame—was necessarily a bad thing, he said: "We all want to say, 'I was here.'"

1913-2005

ROSA PARKS

She refused to give up her seat on a bus, igniting a movement that changed the nation

The 42-year-old seamstress wasn't looking for a fight on Dec. 1, 1955, when she paid her 10-cent fare and took a seat in the fifth row in the "colored" section of a Montgomery, Ala., bus. But when the driver ordered her to give up her seat to a white passenger, she didn't move. When he threatened to have her arrested, she said, "You may do that." Jailed for that act of defiance, Rosa Parks sparked a 381-day Montgomery bus boycott led by Rev. Martin Luther King Jr., which ended when the Supreme Court ruled that segregated public transportation was unconstitutional.

Parks, who died Oct. 24 at 92, remained passionately committed to the civil rights movement throughout her long life. Though she never had children (her husband, Raymond, died in 1977), the woman Nelson Mandela once hailed as "the David who challenged Goliath" left countless admirers. Among them was former President Bill Clinton, who called her, simply, "one gutsy woman."

FRANK PERDUE

After failing as a baseball player, he found his calling crying fowl on TV

There were, no doubt, many reasons for Frank Perdue's success; one of the most important, however, could not be taught at Harvard Business School. "The secret to Frank Perdue is very simple," says Bob Garfield, an editor at *Advertising Age*. "He looked and sounded like a chicken. He had a weird authenticity that made you want to believe there was actually something special about his broilers." Perdue, who grew up in Salisbury, Md., tried to dodge destiny. "One thing I didn't want to be was a chicken farmer," he once said. But after attempting a baseball career, he took over his family's farms and hatched scores of television commercials starring himself and his famous tag line: "It takes a tough man to make a tender chicken." (Perdue Farms sales totaled $2.8 billion in 2004.) Perdue, who suffered from Parkinson's disease, died after a brief illness March 31, at 84.

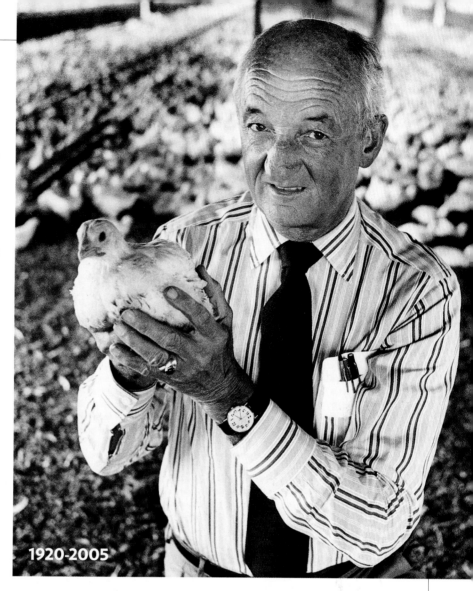

1920-2005

1924-2005

WILLIAM REHNQUIST

When the Chief Justice tilted rightward, the Supreme Court followed

When he walked down the Washington, D.C., streets wearing a newsboy cap and suede Hush Puppies, the Chief Justice of the Supreme Court looked like "the kind of guy you'd expect to see coming out of a bowling alley," said his former clerk Joseph Hoffman. But William Rehnquist left an indelible mark on the court he led for 19 years until his death in September—nearly a year after being diagnosed with thyroid cancer—at 80. A Wisconsin-born conservative who briefly dated Sandra Day O'Connor when the two future justices attended Stanford Law School, Rehnquist remained friendly with even his fiercest ideological court opponents. "He made sure, although they debated with each other, that any nastiness was curbed," said Jay Jorgenson, a former clerk.

2005 INDEX

2005 CREDITS

CONTENTS
(clockwise from top left) Matrix/Bauer-Griffin; Deb Carvalho/FilmMagic; Amanda M. Parks/iPhoto; Allan Grant; Derrick Ceyrac/AFP/Getty; Adam Larkey/ABC; Nigel Parry/CPi, Al Golub/Pool/Zuma; Carolyn Snell/WireImage

HEADLINERS
4-5 Irwin Thompson/Dallas Morning News/Corbis; 6-7 (clockwise from top left) Edmund Fountain/St. Petersburg Times/WPN; Michael S. Wirtz/Philadelphia Inquirer/KRT/Abaca; J Davenport/San Antonio Express/Zuma; David J. Phillip/AP; Eric Gay/AP; David J. Phillip/AP; 8 (top) Suzanne Plunkett/AP; Bay Ismoyo/AFP/Getty; 9 John Russell/The Age/Zuma; 10-11 Khue Bui; 12 Paul Smith/Featureflash/Retna; 14-15 (from left) Johnny Island/INF; Flynet; Andrew Shawaf/Martin Grimes/Pacific Coast News; 16 Nigel Parry/CPi; 17 (top) Khue Bui; Kootenai County Sheriff Dept./AP; 18-19 (clockwise from top left) Courtesy Dove; Bettmann/Corbis; Wolfgang Volz/Laif/Redux; 20 Brian Zak/Gamma; 21 (clockwise from top left) Amanda M. Parks/iPhoto; Limelight Pictures (2); Corrado Giambalvo/AP; 22 Alex Tehrani; 23 (top) Polaris; Robin Nelson/Zuma; 24 Mike Gunnill/AP; 25 Yui Mok/AP; 26 (left) AP (4); Jeff Tuttle/Pool/AP; 27 (top) Chris O'Meara/AP; St. Petersburg Times/WPN; 28-29 Rafiq Maqbool/AP; 30-31 (from left) Paul Buck/EPA; Justin Sullivan/Pool/AP; Steve Griffin/Pool/AP; 32 James White/Corbis Outline; 33 (left) Multnomah County Sheriff's Office (6); Polaris; 34 Ramey; 35 (top) Jerome Maison/Bonne Pioche Productions/Warner; Donato Sardella/WireImage; 36-37 Eric Gaillard/Reuters; 38-39 Axelle/Bauer-Griffin; 40-41 (clockwise from left) Deb Carvalho/FilmMagic; Mike Fanous/Gamma; Damian Dovarganes/AP; 42 (left) Chip East/Reuters; Matt Baron/ BEImages; 43 Kristin Callahan/ Ace Pictures

WEDDINGS
44-47 Maring Photography/Getty (4); (ring) David Rentas/New York Post/Rex USA; 48 Jeff Kravitz/FilmMagic; 49 Joe Buissink/WireImage; 50 (top) Ann Day/ET & The Insider/WPN; Fame; 51 Mark Liddell/Icon Int'l; 52 Ian Jones/Gamma; 53 Nunn Syndication; 54 (clockwise from top left) Brendan Beirne; Reuters/Landov; Dave Hogan/Getty; 55 Yitzhak Dalal; 56 (top) Carlo Allegri/Getty; Splash News; 57 Alex Berliner/BEImages

BABIES
58-59 Marc Royce; 60 INF; 61 Mimi Craven/Icon Int'l; 62 Andrew Southam; 63 Fergus Greer; 64 Courtesy Nancy Kerrigan; 65 (clockwise from top) Courtesy Joan Lunden; Simon Ferreira/Startraks; Landov

ENGAGEMENTS
66-67 Kevin Mazur/WireImage; 68 Kevin Parry/WireImage; 69 (clockwise from top left) LDP Images; Allocca Ferreira/Startraks; Richard Young/Rex USA; Chris Weeks/WireImage

SPLITS
70-71 Carolyn Snell/WireImage; 72 (clockwise from top left) Donato Sardella/WireImage; Mavrix Photo; Ramey; 73 (from top) Seth Browarnik/WireImage; Jon Furniss/WireImage; Jane West/INF; 74 Barry Talesnick/Globe; 75 (left) Flynet; MWD/X 17; 76-77 (left) Jim Smeal/BEImages; Frank Micelotta/Getty

BIG SCREEN
78-79 (clockwise from bottom left) Warner Bros. (2); Richard Cartwright/New Line

TELEVISION
80 Adam Larkey/ABC; 81 (top) Michael Muller/MTV; Richard Cartwright/ABC

FINAL BOW
82-83 Frank Micelotta/Getty; 84 Frank Ockenfels/ABC; 85 Art Streiber/Corbis Outline

ENTRANCES
86-87 © 2002 Edward McCain; 88 Alison Dyer/Blur; 89 Chris Gordaneer

CLASS OF '05
90 Shawn/X 17; 91 (clockwise from center) INF (2); Flynet; John Sciulli/WireImage; 92 (clockwise from bottom left) Gregory Pace/FilmMagic; Flynet; Alex Berliner/BEImages; Fame; 93 Kevin Mazur/WireImage; (inset) Jen Lowery/London Features

FASHION
95 Gilbert Flores/Celebrity Photo; 96-97 (from left) Lester Cohen/WireImage; Stewart Cook/Rex USA; Lisa Rose/JPI (2); Scott Downie/Celebrity Photo; Marcocchi Giulio/Niviere/Sipa; 98-99 (from left) Tammie Arroyo/AFF; Robert Galbraith/Reuters; Tammie Arroyo/AFF; Paul Smith/Retna; Carlos Diaz/INF; Hahn-Khayat/Abaca; 100-101 (from left) Axelle/Bauer-Griffin (2); Brian Lowe/JPI; Tsuni/Gamma; Sara De Boer/Retna; Frazer Harrison/Getty; 102-103 (from left) Rex USA; Jon Kopaloff/FilmMagic; DPA/Landov; Tammie Arroyo/AFF; Nguyen/London Features; INF; 104-105 Erik C. Pendzich/Rex USA; Roger Wong; Dimitrios Kambouris/WireImage; Axelle/Bauer-Griffin; J. Graylock/JPI; Axelle/Bauer-Griffin; 106-107 (from left) Fitzroy Barrett/Globe; Sara De Boer/Retna; Gregg DeGuire/WireImage; Sara De Boer/Retna; Jeff Kravitz/FilmMagic; Alain Rolland/ReflexNews; 108-109 (clockwise from left) Fame; Anthony G. Moore/Globe; Adams-Cousart-Rilloraza/JFX; Tom McGourty/Splash News; Djamilla Rosa Cochran/WireImage

HELPERS
110-111 UNHCR/EPA/Landov; (inset) Reuters; 112-113 (clockwise from top left) Courtesy Petra Nemcova; J. Tayloe Emery/Getty; Stephen Shames/Polaris; Courtesy Jenna Morasca; Chaiwat Subprasom/Reuters/Landov; Lely Djuhari/UNICEF

TRIBUTES
114-115 Allan Grant; 116-117 (clockwise from top left) Anthony Stark Collection; Photofest; Carson Productions/Zuma; Everett; 118-119 Francois Lochon/Gamma; 120-121 MPTV; 122-123 Kwaku Alston/Corbis Outline; 124-125 ABC/Getty; 126-127 (clockwise from top left) ABC Photo Archives (2); Screen Scenes; Steve Fenn/ABC; 128 Terry Arthur; 129 Paul Harris/Globe; 130 UPPA/Zuma; 131 (top) Vince Bucci/Pool/Reuters; Gerard Rancinan/Polaris; 132 (top) Helayne Seidman; Truman Moore/Time Life Pictures/Getty; 133 Marianne Barcellona; 134 Paul Schutzer/Time Life Pictures/Getty; 135 (top) Christopher Ameruoso; AP; 136-137 (clockwise from top left) Gabi Rona/MPTV; Everett; Photofest/Retna; CBS/Landov; Globe; 138-139 (left) Howell Conant/Bob Adelman Books; Phillip Parker; 140 AP; 141 (from top) Terry Arthur; Jason Reed/Reuters

INDEX
143 Albert Ferreira/Startraks

COVER:
(clockwise from top left) Herb Ball/MPTV; Nigel Parry/CPi; Arnold Turner/WireImage; Alex Berliner/BEImages; Bill Davila/Startraks; Gilbert Flores/Celebrity Photo

BACK COVER
(clockwise from top left) Carlos Barria/Reuters; George Pimentel/WireImage; Tony Barson/WireImage; Francois Lochon/Gamma